Major

ROBERT TAYLOR

HAUS PUBLISHING · LONDON

First published in Great Britain in 2006 by
Haus Publishing Limited
26 Cadogan Court
Draycott Avenue
London SW3 3BX

www.hauspublishing.co.uk

A CIP catalogue record for this book is available from the British Library

ISBN 1-904950-72-8

Designed by BrillDesign
Typeset in Garamond 3 by MacGuru Ltd
info@macguru.org.uk

Printed and bound by Graphicom, Vicenza

Front cover: John Holder

Contents

Preface   vi

Part One: THE LIFE
Chapter 1: An Extraordinary Ordinary Man   1

Part Two: THE LEADERSHIP
Chapter 2: Son of Thatcher or Funny Old Tory?   23
Chapter 3: In the Prime of Political Life   35
Chapter 4: The Beginning of the End   62
Chapter 5: Substance without Style   74
Chapter 6: Facing Ethnic Nationalism   87
Chapter 7: The Road to Oblivion   104

Part Three: THE LEGACY
Chapter 8: Major – the Audit   115

Notes   128
Chronology   135
Further Reading   142
Picture Sources   146
Index   148

Preface

Many friends laughed when I told them I had been commissioned to write a short biography of John Major in a series on 20th-century British Prime Ministers. 'You certainly drew the short straw', some exclaimed. In their unthinking attitude to the man they gave uncomfortable confirmation to a widely-held view of John Major. He was still too often regarded as a rather pathetic, grey and earnest figure, the Mr Pooter of modern British politics with a peculiar elocution and the use of quixotic turns of phrase (*fine words butter no parsnips*) that invited mockery rather than empathy. He was seen as a weak and indecisive Prime Minister without any strong convictions of his own. Out of his depth, Major was also viewed as a decent and honourable man but with severely limited abilities. As so often, the conventional wisdom is quite wrong. Major was emphatically not a one-dimensional figure. His longish period as Prime Minister from November 1990 to May 1997 was much more substantial and interesting than the narrow focus provided by an almost overwhelmingly hostile mass media to sleaze and alleged incompetence would suggest. Indeed, it is not difficult to understand Major's obsessive dislike of the newspaper coverage he received during almost all his years in 10 Downing Street. Perhaps more than any other 20th-century British Prime Minister he became the victim of a relentless campaign of denigration and ridicule that ought to tell us far more about the febrile and malicious character of too much of the British political class than the strengths and weaknesses that he displayed while he was in office.

This book is therefore an attempt to understand and explain John Major and to place his premiership in the wider context of modern British politics and the history of the Conservative Party. I have never been a Conservative. Nor have I ever voted for the party in a general election. Over 30 years ago, however, I wrote a short biography of the third Marquess of Salisbury, one of the most successful Conservative Prime Ministers. Ever since I have continued to take a life-long scholarly interest in the Conservatives and in particular to try and understand why it was until quite recently that they were one of the most successful mass political parties in the democratic world.

I did not approach this biography with any bias one way or the other within the context of Conservative partisanship. It is, on the contrary, an attempt to make a balanced assessment of John Major as Prime Minister in the difficult circumstances of his times. As a result I have reached the perhaps unfashionable conclusion that he was a much more important and complicated transitional figure than his many enemies and rivals liked to suggest.

Major does not deserve to be treated either as a political embarrassment or an intellectual lightweight, let alone a figure of fun. Nor should his six and a half years as Prime Minister be dismissed as an utter failure or as an unmitigated disaster. It is true that Major's particular version of compassionate Conservatism failed to find much sympathy or understanding within his own party, let alone across the wider political class. An uncomfortably wide gulf was to exist between his well-meaning if nostalgic, sympathetic rhetoric and the realities of 'Cool Britannia' in the 1990s. Nevertheless, in my overall assessment of Major I hope to challenge those who have either sought to airbrush him out of British history or to treat him almost as a non-person, whose governments were squeezed for a short and unlamented time between the reign of those titans of the modern world – Margaret Thatcher and Tony Blair.

Part One

THE LIFE

Chapter 1: An Extraordinary Ordinary Man

'Does he really exist?'[1] The cruel question asked by the then elderly Conservative Enoch Powell shortly before his death reflected a sneering attitude of patronising condescension and pity that many commentators and fellow politicians were to adopt towards Britain's last Conservative Prime Minister of the 20th century. John Major was turned into a hapless creature of ridicule and contempt, both among a substantial section of his own party and across the metropolitan media elite. There were a few honourable exceptions among political journalists, most notably Matthew Parris and Bruce Anderson, who both expressed sympathy and understanding. The prejudices on display were ably assisted by a persistent chorus of personal abuse and derision that was partly orchestrated by the New Labour spin machine, once Tony Blair was elected Labour Party leader in July 1994. During his last four and a half years as Prime Minister, Major never seemed able to free himself from endless trouble with a substantial number of his backbenchers in the Conservative parliamentary party. He was buffeted by a seemingly bewildering hurricane of adverse events at home and abroad, which added to a growing sense that Major was nothing but a helpless and unlucky figure, unable to assert the authority, discipline, respect and power that he needed over his government and party to become an effective Prime Minister. He was portrayed invariably as grey and mediocre, a pathetic and ultimately a sad and tragic man without any charisma or vision who was reputed wrongly to tuck his shirttails inside his Y-fronts. Major was seen as a strangely limited and one-dimensional figure, out of place in the 'Cool Britannia' of the 1990s with its meretricious cult of youth and permanent obsession with superficial forms of modernisation. It is true that cartoonists like Steve Bell in the *Guardian* did not demonise him as they were to do to Tony Blair, complete with his mad staring eyes, big ears and manic grin. There was rarely any apparent hatred on display towards Major in cartoons as there would be for Blair but on the other hand few signs of much affection were apparent towards him either. Major was often described as a very ordinary man who had 'risen without trace' and that as Prime Minister he held a position which was simply far beyond his intellectual abilities to perform even adequately.

Negative opinions about Major were common during his years in 10 Downing Street. They severely affected his public opinion poll ratings which fell to some of the lowest ever recorded for a serving Prime Minister after September 1992. Although never dropping below those achieved by the Conservative Party, they indicated that he had become a highly unpopular figure among ordinary people beyond the introspective Westminster village during the final years of his government. After an abrupt but dignified retirement from frontline politics after his election defeat in May 1997, Major's reputation failed to stage much of a recovery. Increasingly his period as Prime Minister was seen as an embarrassing and unsuccessful interlude that separated the more substantial Age of Margaret Thatcher from that of Tony Blair. But this over-familiar picture does a grave injustice to John Major. In many important ways he was an extraordinary,

ordinary man whose period as Prime Minister deserves to be treated in its own terms and with more compassion and a deeper understanding of what he faced and what he sought to achieve during his years in Downing Street.

A number of important historical facts about him remained indisputable. Major enjoyed a longer consecutive period as Prime Minister than any other Conservative before him – except for Margaret Thatcher – since Lord Liverpool who ruled Britain for much of the first quarter of the 19th century. Moreover, he spent more time as Conservative Prime Minister than Arthur Balfour, Andrew Bonar Law, Neville Chamberlain, Sir Alec Douglas-Home and Edward Heath. At the age of only 47 he was also the youngest Prime Minister to form a government since the Liberal Lord Rosebery in 1894. Only Tony Blair who succeeded him during the last century was younger when he entered Downing Street. Major was also the only 20th-century Conservative leader who never ran his party in parliamentary opposition.

More significantly perhaps, he could claim with good reason to have won his party the March 1992 general election almost single-handed and in the face of a barrage of pessimistic forecasts from public opinion surveys and media commentators. They had expected and predicted a Labour win or at best for the Conservatives to secure a hung parliament with no party holding an overall majority of seats in the House of Commons. In achieving his own personal triumph against political adversity, Major led what ought to have been a grateful Conservative Party as more than 14 million people voted for them in the election. This was substantially more than Blair ever achieved in his three successive landslide victories – measured in votes – between 1997 and 2005 or Margaret Thatcher in what were her three deceptively easy triumphs. Of course, it is also true that in stark contrast to this high point of success Major went on to preside in May 1997 over the worst electoral defeat inflicted on the Conservatives since well before the 1832 Reform Act. But as he explained in his highly readable and revealing autobiography, by the time he dissolved Parliament even the Archangel Gabriel could not have won a general election for his party.

Major conceded defeat to what was the New Labour Party with his self-respect and integrity intact. As he took his departure, he made a short and poignant statement. *As I leave this morning, I can say with some accuracy that the country is in far better shape than when I entered Downing Street. The economy is booming, interest rates and inflation are low and unemployment is falling. The growth is well set, the health service is expanding, the education service is improving and the crime statistics are falling. The incoming government – to whom I repeat my warm congratulations on their success – will inherit the most benevolent set of economic statistics since before the First World War. I hope very much in the interests of the whole British nation that they are successful.*[2]

The difference in the circumstances that greeted his own arrival as Prime Minister six and a half years earlier on 28 November 1990 could not have proved to be starker. On that occasion, Major had spoken to the nation for the first time outside the front door of 10 Downing Street. It was then that he pledged his ultimate purpose in government would be to create a Britain *that was at ease with itself. I don't promise you it will be easy and I don't promise you it will be quick but I believe it to be an immensely worthwhile job to do. Because it will be neither easy nor quick – if you will forgive me – I will go into Number 10 straight away and make a start right now.*[3]

Major described the wretched legacy waiting for him in his memoirs: *My inheritance was unpromising. We were on the eve of a war. The economic bubble of the 1980s was bursting. Inflation was approaching double figures. Interest rates were at 14 per cent.*

Unemployment had begun to rise by 50,000 a month. House prices were falling. The economy was in the first phase of acute recession.[4]

Major's journey to the door of 10 Downing Street was one of the most astonishing in modern British history. Nobody of such humble social origins had ever before become Prime Minister, with the exception of Labour's Ramsay MacDonald, the illegitimate son of a Scottish crofter who had presided over two short-lived Labour minority administrations between the wars and then a longer time as Prime Minister of a National Government between 1931 and 1935. Even more surprisingly, Major was elected as Conservative Prime Minister in a democratic contest through the secret ballot by a substantial number of his colleagues in the parliamentary party, which was composed overwhelmingly of wealthy, middle class, public school and university educated men – quite unlike himself.

He was born on 29 March 1943 in St Helier Hospital, Carshalton in the Surrey commuter belt, the second son of Tom Major, who was already 63 at the time of his arrival. Major's early childhood years were spent in Worcester Park, where his family lived in a modest four-roomed bungalow in Longfellow Road. He was not born into the manual working class and later he described his family circumstances as *comfortable but not well off*. But he came from a colourful and indeterminate social background which was both uncertain and insecure. His father had once been a music-hall entertainer and a trapeze artist. In the early 1930s he established his own small business, modelling animals and making garden ornaments including gnomes. In the post-war years the Major small enterprise fell on hard times and eventually collapsed. Major's father began to suffer from growing ill health. In his final years he was blind and needed to be cared for. Major's schooldays were, however, uneventful. He passed the 11-plus examination in 1954 and went to Rutlish Grammar School in nearby Merton. But at his father's insistence and against his own wishes, he did so under the name of John Major-Ball. Major had been his father's stage surname and his real one was Ball. The hyphenated name he was compelled to carry with him to the grammar school troubled Major who saw it as an unnecessary burden that he feared would make him look ridiculous to his fellow schoolboys. As a result he approached secondary education *with a wary unease. I believed I would have to excel at sport and be prepared to use my fists to earn the respect of my peers*, he later recalled as he felt he was *sailing under false colours*.[5] Life at home grew more difficult as well as the family fortunes went into decline. In May 1955 the Majors were compelled to move from suburban Worcester Park to a rented two-room top floor flat in a four-storey Victorian building in Coldharbour Lane in the inner-city area of Brixton. They had to share a cooker and they had no bathroom for their own exclusive use. Other tenants included a cat-burglar and a Jamaican with his white girlfriend. The young teenager remembered walking to Dulwich Village and *looking at smart houses with a warm glow through their curtains*.[6] That comfort-able family experience was not for him. The Major family were *stoical in the face of all adversity* but they never lost hope even as their personal circumstances grew more problematic. The young John remained at Rutlish school but his daily journey there was a marathon. It used to take him three hours travel a day six days a week to get there and back from home. His time in secondary education did not turn out to be an academic success. He admitted that he *did as little work as possible* and that the school was *a penance to be endured*.[7] It was there that he learned to play cricket, although not very well, but it was the quintessentially English sport that he came quickly to love for life. Major claimed that the game gave him *some of his happiest moments* and he liked nothing better during the summer holidays than to go and watch Surrey playing at The Oval. On the very afternoon after his resignation as Prime Minister in May 1997, Major travelled to the cricket ground to see his favourite county side in action. His academic performance was, however, undistinguished. Major passed in only three subjects at Ordinary Level – History, English Language and English Literature. *It was a moment of deep shame*, he confessed in his memoirs.[8]

Major left school at the age of 16, seemingly a failure and with few apparent prospects of much success in the adult world of work. His first job he took was as a clerk at the insurance broking firm of Price Forbes near London Bridge, which he disliked intensely. He then joined his elder brother Terry as they tried to develop a garden ornament business like their father had done before them. But by that time Major had another side to his life. He began to develop a keen interest in politics. Major was much encouraged in such precocity by the Labour MP for Brixton, Colonel Marcus Lipton, who gave him a gallery pass to hear the committee stage of the 1956 budget. Perhaps surprisingly Major did not join the Labour party. Instead he became a member of the Young Conservatives. It did nothing initially to improve his employment prospects. In 1963 Major experienced lack of paid work for five months. He was even turned down for a job as a bus conductor with London Transport on the grounds that he was too tall. Eventually he found work with the London Electricity Board in their offices in the Elephant and Castle – close to where he was later to serve as a junior minister in the Department of Health and Social Security. But by now politics was consuming much of Major's leisure time. His aspiration to become a Conservative MP turned out to be a strong motivator in his single-minded determination to launch a sustained effort of educational self-improvement. *I knew that if I were to have a good chance of being selected as a Conservative candidate for Parliament I had to obtain a professional qualification as well as a political profile*, he explained.[9] But Major realised he was already too old to gain the examination results he needed to set out on a conventional university education while he lacked the private financial means to be articled either in the law or accountancy. In the end, he decided to take evening classes in banking. Major joined the District Bank in May 1965 and within 16 months had won his banking diploma.

I knew that if I were to have a good chance of being selected as a Conservative candidate for Parliament I had to obtain a professional qualification as well as a political profile.

MAJOR

He then secured a job with the Standard Bank Group and the alluring promise of working for them overseas. In December 1966 the bank sent him to work for them in the town of Jos in northern Nigeria. Major was not to remain there very long. After only five months he was involved in a serious car accident and broke his left leg in several places. Major was to be troubled permanently by that shattered leg. It afflicted him with a permanent limp and he often found he needed injections to alleviate the pain.

Back home once more, however, Major's political advancement as a Conservative suddenly began to flourish. He had stood unsuccessfully for the party in a ward in Labour-controlled Lambeth in 1964. But his activities were well appreciated by local Conservatives in what was a Labour stronghold. Through hard work and a natural ability to get on well with people, he was elected treasurer of the Brixton Conservative Association. In May 1968 – a year of Conservative landslide council elections nationally – Major also won the normally rock-solid Labour ward of Ferndale on Lambeth Council. At the age of 25 Major he was made deputy chairman of the council's housing committee as well as vice president of the local Conservative Association. It was also at that time that he met and married the 'opera mad' Norma Johnson on 3 October 1970. She was to bring a much needed stability and sense of order to his rather chaotic life and provided him with the supportive, emotional strength that he was to need during his political career. Major was not a Conservative councillor for very long but during his time at Lambeth Town Hall he impressed a young radical Labour contemporary on the council, Ken Livingstone, who later became Mayor of London. Livingstone thought that Major was surprisingly progressive, especially on housing issues and an anti-racist Conservative. But his life as a councillor proved to be short-lived. In May 1971 he failed to win a ward seat in Clapham as Labour recaptured control of Lambeth Council.

By now Major's ambitions rose higher than local government work. He was keen on pressing his claim for a parliamentary nomination. With the support of Jill Knight, the right-wing Birmingham Edgbaston MP, he secured a place on the party's Central Office list of approved candidates. As a result he won the Conservative nomination to contest the safe Labour seat of St Pancras North in the February 1974 general election. He also fought the same constituency and again unsuccessfully in the second election of the year that took place in October. His two inevitable defeats in an inner London seat did not, however, diminish his wish to be elected as a Conservative MP. Major now underwent an exhausting round of applications and interviews as he searched for a winnable constituency for the next general election whenever it came. By this time his career at Standard Charter was also flourishing. The bank's chairman Tony Barber, who had been Edward Heath's Chancellor of the Exchequer in the early

1970s, took him as his personal assistant to an International Monetary Fund conference in Manila. It is possible that Barber used some of his own influence in helping to further Major's political ambitions in the Conservative Party.

Major's breakthrough came eventually in Huntingdon, a safe Conservative constituency in the east Midlands. He defeated nearly 300 aspiring candidates who applied to replace Sir David Renton when he decided to retire, including the future Cabinet ministers Peter Brooke, Chris Patten and Peter Lilley as well as the later Conservative leader Michael Howard. At the final selection meeting Major beat Jock Bruce-Gardyne, Alan Haselhurst and Lord Douro for the nomination. It was an astonishing achievement for the young man from Coldharbour Lane. This certainly seemed to reflect what appeared to be a growing tolerance among some local Conservative Associations about the social origins of prospective candidates. Perhaps the arrival of aspiring families from inner London to the town made the real difference. Major was duly returned as MP for Huntingdon in the May 1979 general election as the Conservatives swept back to power under Margaret Thatcher's populist leadership.

During his first two years in the House of Commons Major remained in the relative obscurity of the Conservative backbenches. He displayed competent abilities, a friendly and engaging personality, as well as a conscientious and diligent way of working. He was certainly not over-awed by life in the House of Commons.

I was as happy as Bunter in a bakery.

MAJOR

I was as happy as Bunter in a bakery, he recalled.[10] But Major was not asked to join the rather exclusive Blue Chip dining club, made up mainly of the new intake of One Nation Conservative MPs who were to be labelled Wets by the Thatcherites. He did not become a member of that club until after the 1983 general election. Perhaps his early exclusion from the club was due to social than political reasons.

Instead Major became a member of the Guy Fawkes Club among backbench Conservatives, which he later described diplomatically as *more workaday* than the Blue Chip. However, in 1981 Major made a breakthrough as he won government recognition for his performances as a loyal and diligent backbencher. He agreed to become unpaid Parliamentary Private Secretary at the Home Office to its two Ministers of State Sir Patrick Mayhew and Timothy Raison. But it was not to be until January 1983 – a few months before that year's general election – that Major joined the government payroll as an assistant in the Whips' Office under Michael Jopling and later John Wakeham. He was to remain in the Whips' Office for the next two years but it was not to be a barren, inconspicuous time for him. On the contrary, it provided Major with plenty of opportunities to come to know all about his fellow members of the Conservative parliamentary party. *I learned about our colleagues and our opponents; their strengths, their weaknesses, their interests and sometimes their secrets. I came to know the team players and the loners; the able and the dotty.*[11] His time in the Whips' Office also enabled his colleagues to get to know more about him and he left them with a highly favourable impression as affable, discreet, hard-working and perhaps above all else loyal and not a known trouble-maker. Major was noticed favourably by Nigel Lawson, the Chancellor of the Exchequer. He was impressed by the expertise that Major displayed in piloting the 1985 budget through the House of Commons expeditiously. Lawson described Major as 'the pick of the 1979 intake', with 'a relatively unusual combination of mastery of detail and likeable manner'.[12]

But Major feared he may have blighted his career prospects earlier in 1985 when he found himself drawn into a fierce argument with the Prime Minister at her annual lunch with the Whips' Office. Margaret Thatcher wrote in her memoirs about the incident: 'John Major was certainly not known to be on the right of the party during his first days as an MP. When he came as a whip to the annual whips' lunch at Downing Street with the other whips, he disagreed with me about the importance of getting taxation down. He argued that there was no evidence that people would rather pay lower taxes than have better social services. I did not treat him or his argument kindly and some people, I later heard, thought he had ruined his chances of promotion. But in fact I enjoy an argument and when the whips' office suggested he become a junior minister I gave him the job which I myself had done first, dealing with the complex area of pensions and national insurance. If that did not alert him to the realities of social security and the dependency culture, nothing would.'[13]

Major remembered the dispute over that lunch ranged more widely. He said as a whip he felt it was necessary to tell Mrs Thatcher what her backbenchers were saying about the government's overall performance. *They don't like some of our policies*, he told her. *They're worried that capital expenditure is being sacrificed to current spending.* Major proceeded to spell out the *grumbles that every whip present knew were the views of the vast majority of our backbench colleagues.* The Prime Minister grew increasingly angry at what he was saying and *began to chew up the messenger. I thought her behaviour was utterly unreasonable and repeated the message*, but this only made her more furious. Major himself said later that he was *almost beside myself with fury* at the way he was being treated. *It was an extraordinary performance by the Prime Minister and I have not forgotten it*, he wrote in his memoirs.[14] Her husband Denis told him as he left the lunch, clutching a gin and tonic —'She'll have enjoyed that'. Major thought his parliamentary career was in ruins as a result although she apologised to him on the following day for what was characteristic behaviour.

As Margaret Thatcher said, the incident did not hurt his prospects of promotion. A few months later Mrs Thatcher plucked Major out of the relative obscurity of the Whips' Office and gave him a junior post at the Department of Social Security under Norman Fowler. His most onerous task there was to shepherd the complex pension clauses in the Social Security Bill through the House of Commons. In doing this, Major provided further evidence to his seniors of an admired capacity for mastering complex detail in a competent and outwardly stress-free manner. In September 1986 Major was promoted in the same department to become Minister of State under Tony Newton who took over from Fowler. In his new position he was drawn increasingly into the inner sanctum of the Thatcher government as he was required to serve on a number of Cabinet committees. His work continued to impress his senior ministerial colleagues. Lawson, who was never renowned for his willingness to confer praise on others, believed that Major had 'demonstrated an impressive grasp of the complexities of the social security rules and an ability to put the government's case across in a firm, clear and agreeable way'.[15]

Such was Major's personal success with other Conservatives that the Prime Minister decided she wanted to promote him to the position of Chief Whip with a Cabinet seat in the aftermath of her third successive general election victory in May 1987. But Lawson persuaded her against making that change. Instead, he urged her to appoint Major as Chief Secretary under him at the Treasury. The Chancellor argued that Major would make him an excellent number two. 'It is ironic that, had he instead become Chief Whip as Margaret had intended, he could never have been a candidate to succeed her when she stepped down in 1990', he wrote later.

Major was not to disappoint Lawson's high personal regard for him. But initially the Chancellor was not particularly impressed by the abilities of his protégé to cope at the Treasury. 'For a time I was concerned that I might have made the wrong choice of Chief Secretary after all – a view I suspect that was shared by John Major himself,' Lawson confessed in his memoirs. 'He found the job far more difficult than anything he had ever done before and had to work very hard to try and master it. He would come and see me at Number 11 ashen faced, to unburden himself of his worries and to seek my advice. Before too long, however, he was thoroughly on top of the job.'[16] It was Major's main task as Chief Secretary to oversee the annual public expenditure round and persuade ministers of the need for cuts and restraint in their departmental spending plans.

> **Nigel Lawson** (b. 1932) entered Parliament in 1974 as Conservative member for Blaby. He was appointed Financial Secretary to the Treasury in the first Thatcher government, and became Energy Secretary in 1981. After the 1983 election he was made Chancellor of the Exchequer, and held the post until 1989, making him the longest-serving Chancellor between Lloyd George and Gordon Brown. Differences with the Prime Minister and her advisers lead to his resignation. He stood down from Parliament at the 1992 general election. He is the father of the cookery writer Nigella Lawson.

This arduous and usually thankless work was exhausting and often painful. As Chief Secretary he had to negotiate the detail of budget allocations that would somehow attempt to reconcile Treasury demands for restraint with departmental efforts to maximise spending opportunities. Major found the experience of those years proved to be invaluable in his later time as Prime Minister.

The work that he had to undertake at the Treasury was often very dull and detailed but Major went about his tasks with a relish. However, as Lawson pointed out his job did not require him to take any personal involvement in the wider public debate about the direction of the government's macro-economic policy that was starting to consume and strain the relations between the Prime Minister and her Chancellor. The role of the Chief Secretary needed administrative and personal qualities of firmness and calmness to keep a tight control on government spending and to ensure money allocated was well spent. It was the kind of tedious work that Mrs Thatcher appreciated and she liked the way Major achieved his aims with his Cabinet colleagues without any fuss or much tiresome conflict. Lawson noticed, however, that Major made sure that he did not intervene in any discussions in the Treasury or in the Cabinet that did not contain a public expenditure dimension. His uncanny ability to keep well away from the big economic issues that increasingly divided Mrs Thatcher from Lawson certainly ensured that Major was not regarded by the Prime Minister as an opponent or any kind of threat to her ideas and policies. Whatever his private feelings might have been, he did not side openly with or against Lawson in a manner that would have antagonised her towards him.

But it was the next sudden step in what seemed like the relentless and upward advance of John Major through the government's ranks that shook the political world. In July

> 'He {Major} found the job far more difficult than anything he had ever done before and had to work very hard to try and master it…. Before too long, however, he was thoroughly on top of the job.'
>
> NIGEL LAWSON

1989 the Prime Minister made him her Foreign Secretary after her brutal demotion of Sir Geoffrey Howe from the post to become Leader of the House of Commons and nominally Deputy Prime Minister. This was the result of growing disagreements over Europe. Major was both surprised and unprepared for such a sudden promotion. He even tried unsuccessfully to argue Mrs Thatcher out of her decision. But she refused to change her mind. She told him she wanted somebody running the Foreign Office that she despised 'who thinks like I do'.[17] Major later described his appointment as *an extravagant gesture of support* from the Prime Minister. But he remained doubtful and reluctant about taking on a post that seemed to over-awe him. Indeed, Douglas Hurd, a former senior civil servant at the Foreign Office and at the time the Home Secretary, who coveted becoming Foreign Secretary himself, spent most of the first day that Major was in his new job trying to persuade him it was 'not such an awful place as he supposed'.[18] Major seemed so overwhelmed by what he saw as the grandeur of the Foreign Office that he moved himself to a small anteroom next to the Private Office that was normally occupied by the Foreign Secretary in order to carry out his work. Mrs Thatcher's chief adviser Charles Powell teased

Born in 1930, Douglas Hurd was Secretary of State for Northern Ireland during the last Thatcher government, and then Home Secretary until replacing John Major at the Foreign Office in 1989. He supported Margaret Thatcher in the 1990 leadership election, but after her withdrawl he himself stood against Heseltine and Major, coming third. He continued as Foreign Secretary under Major until he retired in 1995, seeing the end of the Cold War, the invasion of Kuwait and the wars in the Balkans. He left the Commons in 1997 and was ennobled as Baron Hurd of Westwell.

him on his unlikely appointment by questioning him on his knowledge of geography. 'What's the capital of Colombia?' he asked Major. *Bogota, Charles*, retorted the new Foreign Secretary. *I've been there years ago*.[19] His promotion at least did something to improve his public profile in the outside world. An opinion survey carried out in *The Economist* magazine at the time found only 2 per cent of people had ever heard of him before.

Major proved to be an uneasy and insecure Foreign Secretary but for only 94 days. It was hardly sufficient time to begin to get to grips with the huge workload, let alone to find his feet in such a challenging and high-profile job. But he was able to make a few decisions. One of the most important was to win cabinet approval to stop the sale of British Aerospace Hawk aircraft to Saddam Hussein's Iraq because of its appalling human rights record. His only other substantial contribution was to attend the Kuala Lumpur conference of the Commonwealth heads of government. He thought he was helping Mrs Thatcher to reach an understanding on the application of sanctions against apartheid South Africa but she adopted a more hostile stance in resistance to pressure from Commonwealth leaders and without his involvement. On 26 October 1989 soon after their return from Singapore the Prime Minister summoned Major to Downing Street to tell him he was to become her next Chancellor of the Exchequer. This decision followed her very public squabble with Nigel Lawson and his subsequent resignation over the role of her economic adviser in Downing Street Professor Sir Alan Walters. The Chancellor believed the Professor was exercising an unduly powerful and negative intellectual influence over the Prime Minister on her economic opinions and as a result her sporadic interventions on monetary policy were becoming intolerable to him. Major readily agreed to the job change. He felt much more at ease with himself in returning to the Treasury although he disliked the canard spread about him at the time that he was nothing more than 'the Prime Minister's alter ego'.

Major's most important achievement during his short time as Chancellor was to help to convince Mrs Thatcher that Britain should join the Exchange Rate Mechanism (ERM) of the European monetary system. Sir Peter Middleton, his Permanent Secretary at the Treasury, explained how Major convinced the Prime Minister of the need to agree to that decision after prolonged resistance to the pressures she had experienced from Lawson and Howe: 'Major went out of his way to be sensitive to what the PM wanted to do and the fact that he was sensitive meant they got on pretty well. It also meant that he got his way on most issues. He played her with all the skill of a fly fisherman after a big and suspicious salmon.'[20]

Major did not see Britain's need to join the ERM as a way of emphasising any positive conviction in the creation of a European monetary union, let alone the introduction of a common European currency. But he honestly believed that ERM membership would bring a necessary financial discipline to the management of the British economy which would as a result help to keep a much firmer control on price movements to ensure monetary stability and stop

'He {Major} played her {the PM} with all the skill of a fly fisherman after a big and suspicious salmon.'

SIR PETER MIDDLETON

rising inflation. But it still took many months of persuasion to convince the Prime Minister of agreeing to a move she had resisted so fiercely when pressed on her by Howe and Lawson. On 5 October 1990, however, Major eventually announced that Britain was joining the ERM. It was a popular decision at the time. He did so with the support of a national consensus stretching across industry and the trade unions as well as including the media and the mainstream political parties. In retrospect, it was argued that the country entered the ERM at far too high an exchange rate of DM2.95 to the pound. Mrs Thatcher consented, perhaps against her own instincts, to the fateful decision but she insisted it could only occur in parallel with a cut in interest rates which was also seen with hindsight to have been a mistake.

Major suggested in his memoirs that he held different views about economic policy from Lawson. He argued he was more concerned than his predecessor had been with the widening size of the trade gap, that he did not favour an independent Bank of England, disagreed that the pound should shadow the Deutschmark on foreign exchange markets and believed in the need for a strong manufacturing sector. But Major said he was also determined to take a tough line against inflation under the austere slogan – 'if it isn't hurting, it isn't working'. His relations with Mrs Thatcher were as a result to remain warm and collaborative. She appeared to convince herself she had found the right man that she needed to pursue her policies.

But now unexpected events brought about the Prime Minister's sudden political downfall. Her intemperate public outburst in the House of Commons after returning from an European Union summit conference in Rome in November 1990 triggered her demise. On that occasion, she rejected any suggestions there should be a future European monetary union, a more democratic European Parliament or greater European integration. Her negative attitude provoked the immediate resignation of her long-humiliated former Foreign Secretary and now Leader of the House Sir Geoffrey Howe. In a devastating resignation speech Howe repudiated her policies as well as her personal style of government. This in turn precipitated former Defence Secretary Michael Heseltine's decision to challenge Mrs Thatcher for the party leadership. The result of his dramatic intervention led to a political sensation. Although Mrs Thatcher secured 204 votes among Conservative MP's, Heseltine polled as many as 152. Her majority was just two votes short of what she required for an outright victory under the strange, convoluted rules of the parliamentary party that determined the leadership election procedure. As Major noted ruefully her support was greater than he was to receive in his own election for the party leadership and higher than the vote she won in 1975 to defeat Edward Heath and become Conservative leader. After an initial display of public defiance when she declared outside the British embassy in Paris that she would fight to win in a second ballot against Heseltine, Mrs Thatcher was talked out of doing so by key members of her Cabinet and she decided tearfully to resign from the premiership

Throughout the early stage of the unfolding political drama Major was absent from the Westminster scene. He was at home in Huntingdon recovering from an operation to remove an abscess under a wisdom tooth. There is no evidence to believe that he was anything other than loyal to the Prime Minister before the first ballot. Moreover, he agreed in response to a rather peremptory telephone call from Mrs Thatcher that he would second Hurd's nomination of her candidature in a second-round ballot against Heseltine. *Once again I despaired at her style even as I pledged my support*, he

I could not credibly stand aside without giving the impression that I had no stomach for the top job.

MAJOR

wrote later.[21] His formal loyalty to Mrs Thatcher was to prove unnecessary. In her memoirs she suggested his support for her by that stage was less than enthusiastic. As she wrote later in her own memoirs: 'I asked John to second my nomination. There was a moment's silence. The hesitation was palpable. No doubt the operation on John's wisdom tooth was giving him trouble. Then he said that if that was what I wanted yes. Later, when urging my supporters to vote for John for the leadership, I made play of the fact that he did not hesitate. But both of us knew otherwise'.[22]

Nonetheless Major appeared to be a reluctant contender to succeed Mrs Thatcher as party leader and Prime Minister. He gave the distinct impression that it was only after intense pressure from a growing number of Conservative MPs that he agreed at the last moment to challenge Hurd and Heseltine for the party leadership. *I could not credibly stand aside without giving the impression that I had no stomach for the top job*, he confessed. *Unless I wished to be written off in the future as having shrunk from the challenge, I had little choice but to throw my hat into the ring, though I was still not enthusiastic in doing so.*[23] In the event, Major won an impressive 185 votes, with 131 for Heseltine and only 56 for Hurd. Both his opponents then conceded victory to him without the need to hold a second ballot. As a result Major was elected both Conservative leader and Prime Minister.

Part Two

THE LEADERSHIP

Chapter 2: Son of Thatcher or Funny Old Tory?

Perhaps it was only with hindsight that Mrs Thatcher claimed she remained uncertain about the nature of Major's Conservatism and his abilities as a potential Prime Minister just before his election as her successor. After all, it had been her own firm decision to promote him so swiftly to the Foreign Office and then to the Treasury. If she came later to regret what she had done she had nobody else to blame but herself. 'My problem was the lack of a successor whom I could trust both to keep my legacy secure and to build on it,' she wrote in her memoirs. 'I liked John Major and thought that he genuinely shared my approach. But he was relatively untested and his tendency to accept the conventional wisdom had given me pause for thought.'[1] There were no obvious signs of such hesitation in the autumn of 1990, according to others. Her close political ally Nicholas Ridley – then Environment Secretary – suggested Mrs Thatcher believed that Major would provide a safe pair of hands as Prime Minister to both defend and advance her political inheritance. 'She believed he shared all her views,' wrote Ridley. 'He was highly competent and very pleasant. He did not come from the patrician wing of the party. I don't think any particular speech or television performance or especially dazzling episode prompted her to let her mantle fall upon him. But I do remember her saying to me at the time – "he is another one of us".'[2] However, Nigel

Lawson, who had worked more closely with Major at the Treasury, did not see him as a Thatcherite.

Once she recognised she could not be sure that she would be able to win in a second ballot against the hated Heseltine, Mrs Thatcher made a virtue out of necessity and campaigned vigorously for Major. Her close identification with him was undoubtedly the main reason for his victory inside the parliamentary Conservative Party as her wing of the party voted for him solidly. When it was announced that he had won she told Norma Major delightedly; 'It's what I always dreamed of and hoped for.'[3] Neither of the other two candidates seemed suitable to her to become Prime Minister. Moreover, she had reasoned: 'Given time John might grow in stature or someone else might emerge.' Within a few weeks she was grumbling that the party had made a mistake and Major was already unravelling her achievements and betraying her legacy.

His political beliefs suggested, however, that he could hardly be described as a Thatcherite and 'one of us'. During his campaign for the Conservative leadership succession Major gave the distinct impression that he was something of a One Nation Tory whose role model was none other than the charismatic Ian Macleod, an iconic figure in the party's history who had been seen as being on its left wing. At his official campaign launch Major called for *gradualism, practicalism [sic] and common sense* over Europe. More interestingly he spoke up for the cause of blue-collar worker skills and pledged that he wanted to create *a genuinely classless society in which people can rise to whatever their abilities and their good fortune may take them from wherever they start*.[4] Major described his platform as *moderate, perhaps even centre left. No one could have been misled about where I stood.* But it might also be said that many Conservatives – not least Mrs Thatcher herself – felt a sense of betrayal by his later performance as Prime Minister.

Chris Patten, a One Nation Tory himself and a close political friend whom Major controversially appointed as party chairman recalled in his memoirs; 'Major had never been a Thatcher acolyte. In our days together as young backbenchers I cannot remember disagreeing with him about anything very much. He was a moderate Tory, tough on economic issues, generous on social and very, very competent – the best of our generation.'[5] Patten added that her enthusiasm for Major was perhaps also based on her desire not to see a 'smooth man' who was the product of a public school and Oxbridge and a member of the Carlton Club or White's succeed her. Sir Ian Gilmour, the eminent Tory Wet, who Mrs Thatcher had dismissed in a September 1981 Cabinet reshuffle, was less than impressed by his progressive credentials. 'John Major seemed the least prime ministerial and the candidate least endowed with the attributes of leadership, lacking both the achievements and the abilities of his rivals', he argued.[6] Gilmour suggested Major had won the leadership because both the right and the left wings of the party had gained the distinct impression that he was one of them. In this apparent deception he believed that Major revealed a 'lack of strong political views'. Moreover, Gilmour was to suggest he 'made not the smallest attempt to lead his party and his government into the One Nation tradition. Probably the thought never occurred to him'. In his opinion, Major 'kept to the Thatcherite path; in many ways, indeed, his government became even more right wing than hers'.

'He {Major} was a moderate Tory, tough on economic issues, generous on social and very, very competent – the best of our generation.'

CHRIS PATTEN

Major's former mistress Edwina Currie recorded somewhat confusingly in her vengeful published diaries that on one occasion Major had declared to her; 'In some ways I am more

Thatcherite than Thatcher – the mortgage relief she would never have done. But I am not a Thatcherite and never have been'.[7] In the few attempts he made in explaining his Conservative philosophy he could often certainly sound as if he was a man from the left. But then Major was never comfortable with having anything as distinctive as a well-formed and coherent ideology. He often remained uneasy in identifying himself with any particular kind of Conservatism. 'He disliked isms. He liked people. He did not want to make a cult of his own ideas; he believed in the traditional values of his party,' suggested Sarah Hogg and Jonathan Hill, his close Downing Street party advisers in the policy unit he formed. 'He was not fond of change for its own sake.' They were convinced that whatever 'strong convictions' he held they derived from his own personal experiences that he had gained along the long, tough road he travelled from Brixton to Huntingdon. These amounted to 'the dignity of personal ownership and the desire to give people more direct control over bureaucracy'. Such basic instincts underlay 'his hatred of inflation, his commitment to privatisation, to open markets' and it was in this way that he 'shared' the beliefs of his predecessor. As Hogg and Hill explained: 'John Major was sensitive to misfortune, tolerant of diversity and a living example of the "Britain without barriers", the "classless society", "the country at ease with itself" that he wished to create. When he talked of "the power to choose and the right to own", these ideals reflected his own aspirations.' Apparently 'a hand up and not a hand out' was his view of social policy. 'He liked plain English, simple images rooted in tradition and love of country, down to earth objectives and practical policies. He hated pretension and prejudice. He had known from experience what life was like inside a struggling city heap [sic] and wanted to widen the channels of opportunity which Thatcherism had opened up for the toughest and most able.'[8]

Major's Premiership

The 18 months leading up to the general election in 1992 'were the high days of Major's consensual, consultative style in the Cabinet Room and in his bilaterals with ministers. Neither would wholly survive the traumas of late 1992. After that he would bring less and less to full Cabinet for fear of leaks and would skip through the regular business item of European affairs … for fear of the party's civil war on Europe erupting and poisoning the entire proceedings.' … . But it was apparent from the outset of his premiership that Major was a Prime Minister who needed close political friends around him whom he could trust. Graham Bright, his Parliamentary Private Secretary, was very important to him. "Major relied on and trusted" Bright. But the central relationship of 1990–92, to the surprise initially of some, was the Major-Patten axis. Chris Patten remembers Major seeming a young (he was 47) and inexperienced man, saying on his first morning in No.10 "I don't know if I can do this job. I wasn't really expecting it yet." Major made Patten his Party Chairman and he swiftly became, in Anthony Seldon's words, "the political ally who stood out"… . The Prime Minister became increasingly dependent on Patten's advice and friendship. Patten, who had been central to Hurd's leadership campaign, not Major's, in November 1990, said later: 'There was every conceivable reason why he should have mistrusted me, but I don't think I have ever been trusted as much by anybody in my entire life.' Once Patten had lost his Bath seat at the 1992 election and taken the Governorship of Hong Kong, Major pined for his old friend and the phone calls were plentiful from No. 10 to the Governor's Mansion in the autumn of 1992 and beyond as the Prime Minister sought solace and counsel as his troubles intensified. It was plain to his colleagues that Major never found a surrogate for Patten. It is difficult to speculate about the difference Patten might have made had he retained Bath. Major's tranquility index would have been higher. [Peter Hennessy, *The Prime Minister* (Penguin, London: 2000) pp 444, 452.]

My Conservatism came from what I saw, what I felt and what I did, as well as what I read. It shaped what I wanted to do in office, Major wrote in his memoirs. *When I was young my family had depended on the public services. I have never forgotten – and never will – what the National Health Service meant to my parents or the security it gave despite all the harsh blows that life dealt them. Nor have I forgotten the care I received at a critical time after my accident in Nigeria. These personal experiences left me with little tolerance for the lofty ideas of well-cosseted politicians, the metropolitan media or Whitehall bureaucrats who made little use of the public services in their lives and had no concept of their importance to others. They may have looked down on the public sector and despised it as second rate but many of them knew nothing of the people who worked there or the manifold problems they faced.*[9]

Major's Conservatism certainly did not sound much like that of Margaret Thatcher's. *The Conservative Party does not belong to any one individual. The ism I wished to promote was a traditional Conservatism tempered with an understanding of and sympathy for life at many levels.* In his first speech to his party as Prime Minister Major attempted to explain what this meant: *We aim for a society of opportunity – But amidst the inevitable thrust of life it should be a compassionate society. Genuinely compassionate – because some people do need a helping hand to enable them to enjoy a life full of choice and independence.*[10]

Incongruously for a Conservative, Major went on to quote the memorable words of that 17th-century radical Lieutenant Colonel William Rainsborough in the famous Putney debates with the Levellers in 1647: 'I think the poorest he that is in England hath a life to live as the greatest he.' In the speech he made in accepting the party leadership Major set out his vision of the society he wanted to create. *A truly open society – open because we believe that men and women should be able to go as far as their talent, ambition and effort take them. There should be no artificial barriers of background, religion or race. We aim for a society of opportunity where people can better themselves and their families by their own efforts – a Britain that puts people in control of their own lives, to exercise their own choices, in their own time and in their own way.*

Major gave the clear impression that he wanted to create a classless country. In his memoirs he quoted a passage from a speech that he made during his successful 1992 general election campaign that came closest to such a progressive sentiment. *I want to bring into being a different kind of country, to bury forever old divisions in Britain between north and south, blue collar and white collar, polytechnic and university. They're old style, old hat.*[11] Such passionate feelings seemed far removed

We aim for a society of opportunity – But amidst the inevitable thrust of life it should be a compassionate society.

MAJOR

from those of the typical Conservative MP emerging from the Age of Thatcherism. But they were what appeared to motivate Major in his approach to democratic politics. Edwina Currie noted in her diary that in an early speech to the party when Prime Minister Major had sounded very much like a man of the left. She wrote of his 'personal agenda, much of which seems to have been pinched from the socialists'.[12]

He was often mocked for his nostalgic evocation of what sounded like the lost England of the 1950s – *of long shadows on county grounds, warm beer, invincible green suburbs, dog lovers and pool fillers and – as George Orwell once said – old maids bicycling to Holy Communion through the morning mist.*[13] It was as deceptive and misleading a vision of England as the Conservative Prime Minister Stanley Baldwin's own romantic portrait of a lost rural arcadia that he had spoken about in the inter-war years. Major's highly personal but cosy and rather parochial, homespun picture of an idealised country reflected not only his own sentimental attachment to an English past that he had never experienced in his own life but it also pointed to deep and enduring conservative values of love of nation and of family as well as the spirit of community that he believed lay just below the glittering and meretricious surface of modern society. In his speech to the 1993 party conference he sought to explain his commitment to other old values – *neighbourliness, decency, courtesy. It is a time we returned to those core values*, he told his audience. *To get back to self discipline and respect for the law, to consideration for others, to accepting responsibility for yourself and your family and not shuffling it off on other people and the state.*[14] Such sentiments went down well with the ageing Conservative faithful. Uncanny echoes of all of them were to be found in the Respect Agenda that Blair sought briefly to make his big idea during New Labour's third term in government 13 years later.

Born in Liverpool in 1946, Edwina Currie was elected MP for South Derbyshire in 1983. In 1986 she became a junior health minister in the Conservative government, but was forced to resign two years later over a warning about salmonella in eggs which was felt by the industry to go too far. She lost her seat in the 1997 general election. She has written six novels and from 1998 to 2003 hosted a radio talk show. In 2002 she published her diaries, which revealed her four-year affair with John Major (1984 to 1988).

But Major's Conservatism also contained a strong ingredient that also appealed to his party and to a wider audience. He was an unashamed Unionist. Major remained firmly opposed to any devolution in self-government to Scotland and Wales, that both Labour and the Liberal Democrats favoured. His commitment to Unionism, of a United Kingdom, was unyielding and something he would not compromise on. In the 1992 general election campaign and again in 1997 Major made his government's defence of the Union a key theme even though it was an issue in Scotland that antagonised rather than won over potential voters to the Conservative Party.

The most perceptive appreciation of Major's rather nostalgic but also inchoate political beliefs came from the Conservative columnist Matthew Parris. 'Ideologically he was never in Tory terms, remotely a Thatcherite or even a centrist,' he wrote. 'More than once when the argument was about state spending and state intervention, John was way to the left of many of us and certainly me in his belief in the role of the state. He saw this role as the protector of the weak, empowerer of merit where merit lacked muscle and preserver and promoter of social balance.'[15] It is doubtful whether anybody else in the higher reaches of his party, let alone the increasingly ageing rank-and-file, shared Major's vision of such a curiously old-fashioned but vaguely compassionate Conservatism. Even Parris admitted that he did not agree with what Major appeared to believe in.

'Ideologically he {Major} was never in Tory terms, remotely a Thatcherite or even a centrist.'

MATTHEW PARRIS

But the lack of either sympathy or understanding for Major's personal agenda also reflected the harsh spirit of the times. Britain in the 1990s was not the kind of country that Major yearned for. Nor was there much real possibility that it could be turned into one in which he could have ever felt at ease with himself. The Age of Thatcherism did much to destroy the concept of civil society and undermine autonomous and voluntary associations beyond the family. It also denigrated the professionalism of the public service ethic and any commitment to a benign but necessary state that sought to include and embrace all of its citizens. Mrs Thatcher had fought with some success to eradicate the so-called post-war social and economic settlement that had shaped British politics for more than 30 years. She dismantled not only much of the state sector in industry but successfully confronted and weakened trade union power and sought to liberate the ambitious and the enterprising from the burden of high taxes and over-regulation. Her purpose was to give free rein to an acquisitive and possessive individualism, to encourage the voice of the consumer and not so much the citizen or the producer. She wanted to transform Britain into a vibrant free-market economy and to remove the suffocating state corporatism that she believed had turned the country into the sick man of Europe. There is not much evidence to suggest that Major ever really disagreed at least in public with any of her fundamentalist convictions or the main thrust of her ideological agenda before he became Prime Minister. Indeed, he was himself one of the most prominent beneficiaries of her socio-economic revolution, a man of humble origins who had made it in politics through the new Conservative Party that she was creating.

His often opaque vision of compassionate Conservatism seemed more like a dream than a sentiment that could be turned into a credible programme for government action. Major was not the only modern politician who found it almost impossible to translate the well-meaning rhetoric of his good intentions into practical realities. His own thoughts did not reflect any coherent ideology or recognisable tradition of Conservatism. There was an understandable confusion perhaps within himself over the essential connection that there has to be in politics between means and ends. The gulf between what he evoked and what he delivered was always to be enormous and it widened significantly during his years in 10 Downing Street. The results could not entirely be blamed on the adverse circumstances that came to drag his premiership down into its unfortunate reputation for incompetence and sleaze. They reflected in part the tragic inadequacies of his particular kind of Conservatism. Unfortunately for him the Britain that he came to govern in November 1990 could not be remade into the kind of country in which he had grown up in. The social conformity, the sense of order and hierarchy, the belief in good manners and *esprit de corps*, the commitment to common decency and a gentle patriotism, were no longer acceptable to an increasing number of British people. It is true that the country was still very much a class-dominated society. The years of Margaret Thatcher made the country even more divided by wealth, power and income than it had been before May 1979 but it was also one in which the ambitious and the footloose were able to thrive and where older notions of trust, solidarity and social citizenship no longer resonated. In one important sense, Major's attitude was admirable. He was tolerant of the so-called new morality. He was anti-racist as a man from Brixton might have been expected to be and he disliked gender inequality intensely. He took a more enlightened view of homosexuality than many in his party. He wanted to open up a still class-bound and hierarchical society to all the talents. But his compassionate Conservatism also often seemed confused and contradictory. It was not possible to make Britain more tolerant, diverse and civilised, even less inequitable while at the same time yearning for a return to the conventional conformities that were associated rightly or wrongly with the world of his formative years in Worcester Park and Brixton.

It was therefore a rather untypical and strange Conservative who crossed the threshold into 10 Downing Street on the afternoon of 28 November 1990. However, Major's time as Prime Minister should not be seen as merely an unhappy and undistinguished epilogue after Margaret Thatcher's long reign nor as an irrelevant interlude before the advance and consolidation of her divisive legacy by Tony Blair's New Labour project. Major wanted to lead the Conservatives back to the political centre and restore them to what they regarded to be their proper role as the natural party of government, capable of reassuring the electorate through their administrative competence, pragmatism and moderation. Most Conservatives in November 1990 were sick and tired of what they saw increasingly as the hectoring and hubristic style of Mrs Thatcher, with her restless activism. At one level Major seemed to offer what many of them hankered for at that time – a period of calm and reassurance. But he was also seen by many in the party as a Conservative who had won her trust and support and therefore he held out the promise to them that he would not seek to unravel her achievement but instead to build upon it. Major, in other words, stood at one and the same time for both the forces of consolidation and those of advance. In the words of Chris Patten, the winning political combination in 1990 that attracted so many Conservatives to Major was as the party's representative for 'both continuity and change'.[16] It was with that paradox which Major was compelled to wrestle with during most of his troubled six and a half years as Prime Minister.

In 1991 John Major met with the actor Ian McKellen, representing the gay rights organisation Stonewall, to discuss the issue of the equalisation of the age of consent for homosexual men (set at 21 by the 1967 Sexual Offences Act), signalling a more liberal attitude than under Thatcher. In February 1994 Edwina Currie tabled an amendment to the Criminal Justice Bill to equalise the age of consent, but both the Commons and the Lords rejected this, reducing it to 18 which the government supported. The age of consent was finally equalised in January 2001.

Chapter 3: In the Prime of Political Life

The early weeks of John Major's government were to come as a welcome liberation for his colleagues after the increasingly tense final days of Mrs Thatcher's domination. One member of the Cabinet even likened the feeling to that of the prisoners' chorus in Beethoven's *Fidelio* when they were set free from their dungeon. Douglas Hurd, as Foreign Secretary, described the welcome change of atmosphere that followed Major's sudden arrival in 10 Downing Street: 'No longer did any serious discussion in the cabinet begin with a statement of the Prime Minister's views. John Major usually reserved himself for the summing up before which he took the trouble to ensure that all significant voices round the table had been heard. Of course, the Prime Minister held personal views on most subjects, even if not so absolutely as his predecessor. But he preferred not to overawe opposition with the assumption that it could not exist. Instead he lured it into the open, exposed it to criticism and thus weakened it so that with luck it could be finally disposed of in his summing up.'[1]

Charles Powell, Mrs Thatcher's chief adviser, made a telling contrast in the moods between Mrs Thatcher and Major; 'She was tensed up all the time, highly strung, very active. She would be up at 5.00 a.m., telephoning all hours of the day and night meeting this person and that, saying get this done, never stopping for a moment. John Major has quite a placid temperament. He functioned much better with a more regular life. He needed seven hours' sleep whereas she could cope with three hours a night for weeks at a time and it didn't affect her performance.'[2] In this, Major was very much an ordinary man.

In his revealing memoirs Major explained his own conception of how he intended to behave as Prime Minister: *After the pomp and circumstance of the Thatcher years I was keen to present an antidote to that to show people that it was possible to be prime minister without changing, without losing the interests that every other Briton had, without having no time for holidays, no time for sport, no time for anything but the higher things of life. I wanted to show that it was possible to be prime minister and remain a human being, just like the fifty-five million other human beings in the country but with an exceptional job.*

Major wrote that he went into Downing Street with the clear determination to pursue an open and civilised way of behaviour as Prime Minister.

I wanted to show that it was possible to be prime minister and remain a human being.

MAJOR

Having power reminded me that it needed to be exercised in a way that did not make you different from other people. But I had no problem about exercising the power to order people to do things. It was a tool, a mechanism. Douglas Hurd said to me later that he felt 'I did not enjoy the job' and perhaps he was right. I was brought up to accept obligations as well as rights and I felt this strongly as prime minister. I think I felt quite differently about power than any prime minister this century.[3]

His first Cabinet appointments seemed to reflect his understandable desire to restore some semblance of unity to a divided party. Michael Heseltine was brought in from the cold since his impetuous resignation from Mrs Thatcher's Cabinet in January 1986. He was made Environment Secretary and given the all-important and urgent remit of finding a more credible alternative to replace the rates than the hated and regressive Community Charge ('Poll Tax') which had incensed so many Conservatives and lost Mrs Thatcher significant support among previously loyal backbenchers. Heseltine's return to the Cabinet was not welcome to either Mrs Thatcher or her supporters who all saw his appointment as a provocation. But Major was not to regret that decision later on and he came to value Heseltine's energies and loyalty, especially after he made him Deputy Prime Minister after July 1995 during his second term. The elevation of the left-wing Conservative Chris Patten to the position of Party Chairman was a clear sign of Major's intentions and it was also a move that many on the right of the party resented. Douglas Hurd remained at the Foreign Office. Clearly none of those three big figures could be remotely described as Thatcherites. But Major did appoint Norman Lamont, who had been his campaign manager, as Chancellor of the Exchequer. In his memoirs Major argued that Lamont turned out to be *a better chancellor than he was given credit for* and suggested that *part of his legacy was the excellent economy we would hand over to Tony Blair in 1997.*[4] There were also promotions for the affable Scotsmen – Ian Lang who went to the Scottish Office and Malcolm Rifkind to the Transport Department. Sir Richard Ryder became Chief Whip and David Mellor Chief Secretary to the Treasury. But Major's first Cabinet was more continuity than change. As many as 13 out of its 21 members who had served under Margaret Thatcher remained in place. None of Major's colleagues were, however, women. It was the first time since 1954 that a Cabinet had contained no female member.

But while his more collegial approach and apparent restoration of Cabinet government may have reassured his senior colleagues, Major inherited what looked like a difficult, if not impossible political legacy. The destruction of Margaret Thatcher at the hands of her own party had traumatised many Conservatives. She left behind her a bitterly bruised and divided parliamentary party. Many MPs felt ashamed of what they had done. Some even refused to accept the verdict. Moreover, Mrs Thatcher herself was to do very little to help the man she had virtually anointed as her successor. Major had sought to reassure his party that he wanted to heal the wounds and establish a new unity among the Conservatives. Heseltine's return was an important sign that Major sought a reconciliation with the man who had brought about Mrs Thatcher's downfall. But his predecessor was in no mood for forgiveness and reconciliation. 'I shan't be pulling the levers there but I shall be a very good back-seat driver', she announced. *The comment was not made with malice*, Major wrote later. *But it had a malign effect. It implied after she had left Downing Street she would be making decisions about how things were run – and that was never going to be the case. Her comment ensured that if I continued with policies she had advocated I would simply be regarded as 'the son of Thatcher'; while if I did not, it would be said that I was wrecking her legacy. That, of course, is how it turned out. Her comment forced a wedge between us that was to grow wider as month succeeded month.*[5]

'I shan't be pulling the levers there but I shall be a very good back-seat driver.'

MARGARET THATCHER

His personal style as Prime Minister was not to be abrasive, intolerant, and far from authoritarian. Blair once sneered at Major: 'I lead my party but you follow yours.' That barbed comment hurt him but it was accurate. Major saw himself very much as a healer and a conciliator and not a warrior. This meant not only listening and understanding, with patience and calmness, to what other Conservatives had to say but removing any sense of superiority or personal domination from his work as Prime Minister with his own party. Initially this approach was welcomed by most Conservative back-benchers. But as time passed, it came to be seen not as a sign of strength but of serious weakness. What many Conservatives wanted and perhaps more importantly needed was to feel the smack of firm government. Mrs Thatcher could inculcate loathing but much more important she brought a sense of fear to many in her party. She had wielded executive power in an often ruthless and unreasonable way. Of course, in the end it sealed her downfall. But for long stretches it brought effective results. The contrast with Major was startling.

But during his first 16 months as Prime Minister this did not appear to matter very much. In November 1990 the Conservatives were facing the serious threat of electoral oblivion. The main reason for Thatcher's downfall had been the growing realisation among many Conservative MPs that she would not be able to win them another general election victory. The urgent need for party unity and for rallying around the new Prime Minister was seen as a matter of natural survival. What slim chance Conservatives believed they retained for winning an unprecedented fourth term in government would be achieved only if John Major turned out to be a political success. In fact, his early period in the premiership was surprisingly effective. His very appearance in 10 Downing Street was enough to improve his party's standing in the opinion polls. The mere change of occupant proved dramatic. Now the main political parties were suddenly running neck-and-neck again. The prospect of a Labour election landslide evaporated. The arrival of a new Prime Minister, even a Conservative one, had made a significant difference to the attitude of the electorate. Many voters even seemed to believe a fresh government had actually taken power. After the increasingly shrill and imperious Margaret Thatcher, Major looked like a friendly and competent man with plenty of common sense and a down-to-earth approach to politics. His very ordinariness seemed a genuine electoral asset. Major belonged to the human race. He sounded like a well-meaning pragmatist. Hardly a heroic figure, but he was what a country in recession needed.

But more importantly, Major succeeded in his first short term as Prime Minister in defusing the innumerable problems he found smouldering in his in-tray. The first and most urgent task he faced was the likely launch of a Gulf War to liberate the small sheikhdom of Kuwait from the Iraqi dictator Saddam Hussein's military occupation following his invasion on 2 August 1990. On the very day of Major's first Cabinet meeting, the United Nations Security Council passed a resolution that set a deadline of 15 January 1991 for Saddam to withdraw his troops from Kuwait. It authorised that 'all necessary means' should be taken to remove him from the sheikhdom if he refused to withdraw his army voluntarily. British armed forces were already in the Arabian peninsula alongside the large American and other allied contingents, preparing for an assault. Major lost no time in visiting President George Bush in Washington to establish a close personal relationship with him and to discuss the imminent prospect of war in the Gulf. He was as committed as Margaret Thatcher to the liberation of Kuwait. No real differences of opinion existed

George H W Bush (b. 1924) was the 41st President of the United States and the last Second World War veteran to hold the office. A former congressman, US representative to the UN and to China, and Director of the CIA from 1976 to 1977, he was Ronald Reagan's Vice-President for both of his terms. He defeated the Democrat Michael Dukakis in the 1988 presidential election, losing to Bill Clinton in 1993. He is the father of the US President George W Bush.

between them over the issue. Major and Bush also soon found they enjoyed each other's company on a personal level. The Prime Minister agreed with the American plan for instant aerial attacks on Iraq itself on the day after the UN Security Council deadline expired. Perhaps to his own relief Major did not find Bush vainglorious for war but as calm, firm and resolute as himself that military action would be launched if Saddam did not respond positively to the United Nations ultimatum. The Prime Minister made a Christmas visit to British forces in the Gulf to show support and encouragement for their imminent endeavours. But he did not behave like King Henry V before the battle of Agincourt. Never bombastic, Major avoided hyperbole but he spoke honestly and straightforwardly to the men. *I went to bed with mixed emotions*, he recalled on the night before the assault on the Iraqi forces. *Anticipation of course. Also confidence that we had no choice and were right to act – Above all I wondered what would be in the minds of the young aircraft crews as for the first time they launched themselves into action.*[6] Operation Desert Storm was over in just under two months. After five weeks of intensive aerial attack on Iraq, allied forces drove Saddam's forces out of Kuwait in less than six days. Major agreed with Bush they should not go on to topple Saddam's regime in Iraq. Instead a cease-fire was reached on February 28. In retrospect, Major believed the decision not to march on to Baghdad was the correct one. As he wrote wisely in his memoirs, published nearly four years before the Anglo-American occupation of Iraq and removal of Saddam in March 2003: *There was no UN resolution empowering the allies to go into Baghdad and drag Saddam out by the heels. Nor should the allies have done so even if it had been possible. If the nations had gone to war on the basis of international law were themselves to break that law, what chance would there have been in future of order rather than chaos? What authority in future would the great nations have had against law breakers if they themselves broke the law and exceeded the UN mandate? They would never have been trusted again. No similar coalition could have been formed in the future.*[7]

But Major also launched his own international initiative to ensure that effective protection, through the formation of safe havens, should be provided for the vulnerable Kurdish minority in the north of Iraq who feared Saddam would enforce a policy of genocide against them. The Prime Minister was successful in doing this. He convinced an initially reluctant President Bush to commit American ground troops to aid the Kurds. *Food, water, clothing and shelter were provided on a massive scale*, wrote Major. *Genocide was averted and literally tens of thousands of lives were saved. So too, I think, was the reputation of the allies which would surely have been harmed had we turned a blind eye.*[8] Major's measured and firm performance during the First Gulf War enhanced his own reputation and that of Britain. It was the first part of the troublesome Thatcher legacy that he had handled with a studied finesse and that won him widespread admiration.

> *If the nations had gone to war on the basis of international law were themselves to break that law, what chance would there have been in future of order rather than chaos?*
>
> MAJOR

The second problem he inherited was to prove much more difficult to resolve, although in the short term Major scored something of a personal triumph in dealing with it. Attitudes to the future of the European Union were to divide the Conservatives throughout his period as Prime Minister and far beyond in a way that no other issue was to do. It had helped to bring about Mrs Thatcher's own downfall and it continued to divide and trouble the party after her departure. Although a Conservative government under Edward Heath

The Special Relationship

During Major's term in office Britain showed that, despite its one-sided nature, there was still life in the 'Special Relationship'. Britain was prepared to commit her troops to American missions in a way that her other allies were not. Britain's continued reliance on NATO as the cornerstone of its defence illustrated Major's belief that the US still had a prominent role to play in Europe's security.

In April 1995 Major visited Clinton, and raised the idea of a transatlantic free trade agreement, but received tepidly in Washington. The idea of a North Atlantic trade alliance was gaining support at the time, powerful voices were behind the campaign including Henry Kissinger who called for 'Special Relationship' between the US and Europe, and proposed a North Atlantic Free Trade Group as a economic foundation. Major, then, went beyond trying to cement the Special Relationship between Britain and US, and instead, perhaps released from the constraints of his eurosceptic Cabinet at home, put forth the concept of European trade alliance. There was a sense, on both sides of the Atlantic, that with the Cold War over NATO had served its purpose.

Bill Clinton entered the Northern Ireland peace process despite prominent voices in the US establishment discouraging him from doing so. He almost single-handedly set about changing the United States view of Northern Ireland. In November 1995, with the Downing Street Declaration of 1993 faltering, Clinton visited both Northern Ireland and the Republic, receiving a unanimously rapturous welcome from Catholics and Protestants alike. An international body (or envoy), chaired by a US senator (George Mitchell) was established to encourage all-party talks and to oversee the decommissioning of weapons. This caused some embarrassment for the British Government, which had always seen Northern Ireland as a matter of domestic and internal affairs. In January 1994 Clinton lifted the travel ban on the Sinn Fein leader Gerry Adams. In turn, the Republic lifted the media ban on Sinn Fein. Clinton told the people of Northern Ireland that they were 'making a miracle', but this fragile peace lasted only until 1996 when bombs were detonated in Manchester and London.

had negotiated and taken Britain into what was in 1973 called the European Economic Community, the country remained an awkward and often semi-detached member of an organisation that was as much a political as an economic project for the democratic unification of the continent. Mrs Thatcher had grown in her later years as Prime Minister more irrational and even hysterical in her attitude to Brussels. She began to fear that there were now plans afoot to turn the European Union into a federal state that would bring an end to the national sovereignty of member countries and with it Britain's own independence. Efforts to convince her that the creation of the single European market by 1992 for the free movement of goods, services, labour and capital was very much in line with her own free-market opinions failed to convince Mrs Thatcher, even though she presided over the formation of that single market and agreed to sterling's entry into the European Exchange Rate Mechanism.

Major recognised from the beginning of his premiership the dangers that Europe posed for the Conservatives. *I was standing astride a deep and widening fissure in the party*, he admitted. He saw constantly the shadow of his 19th-century predecessor Sir Robert Peel at his side. *In all my time at Downing Street I was never to leave it*, wrote Major.[9] Peel had split the Conservatives in 1846 when he decided to repeal the protectionist Corn Laws and dealt a blow to the landed interest. A more accurate parallel for Major was perhaps that of Arthur Balfour, Conservative Prime Minister between 1902 and 1905, who tried unsuccessfully to maintain party unity in face of the divisive tariff reform campaign of Joseph Chamberlain that led to a disastrous defeat at the hands of the Liberals in the 1906 general election.

Major was keen at first to make a fresh start on the European question and pursue a more conciliatory approach to other

EU member states. Soon after he became Prime Minister he travelled to Bonn to meet the German Chancellor Helmut Kohl who became an ally, at least to begin with. On that occasion he also made a speech that set out his own positive views on the future of the European Union. *My aim for Britain in the Community can be simply stated*, he told his audience in Germany. *I want us to be where we belong. At the very heart of Europe. Working with our partners in building the future.*[10] But he also made it clear that he would reserve his judgement on whether Britain would agree in future to the creation of a common European currency to replace the national currencies. *Europe is made up of nation states; their vitality and diversity are sources of strength*, he insisted. *The important thing is to strike the right balance between closer co-operation and a proper respect for national institutions and traditions*. His advisers Sarah Hogg and Jonathan Hill pointed out that Major's belief that Britain should be at 'the very heart of Europe' was 'never code for a federalist agenda'.[11] 'It was merely a signal that Britain was going to play an active part' in negotiations on the future of Europe.

In fact, Major saw himself as a genuine pragmatist towards the EU. *I believed it was in our economic interests to be a member. I welcomed sensible co-operation. I had no hang-ups about Germany. I accepted that being one of a Community of fifteen meant that sometimes we had to reach a consensus that was not entirely to our taste*, he wrote of his early dealings with the Continent as Prime Minister. *I was keen to rebuild shattered fences, to prevent Britain from being seen for ever as the odd man out to be excluded from the private consultations that so often foreshadowed new policy in Europe.*[12]

> *I was keen to rebuild shattered fences, to prevent Britain from being seen for ever as the odd man out to be excluded from the private consultations that so often foreshadowed new policy in Europe.*
>
> MAJOR

Major showed what this meant in his shrewd handling of his government's negotiations on the EU's Maastricht treaty in December 1991. The proposed document was to set out the next stage in the EU's evolution but it was hardly the blue-print for a centralised and authoritarian state that an increasing number of Conservatives seemed to fear was being planned. The Prime Minister explained to the House of Commons what his position would be before the negotiations began at Maastricht with Britain's EU partners. He made it clear he would oppose any commitment to the creation of a federal union in Europe. Nor would there be any support from Britain for compulsion in the introduction of a common European currency or a monetary union. Foreign and interior policies were not going to be subordinated to a supra-national authority in Brussels either. In addition, Britain would not swallow any social chapter in the proposed new treaty that would extend employment regulations to the country that Major believed might undermine its competitiveness on global markets and encourage a return of trade union power. Major was not, however, entirely negative in his attitude to the EU. He was prepared to concede that more power should be given to the European Parliament to investigate cases of alleged fraud inside the Community and he wanted to ensure that the European Court of Justice would abolish state subsidies that he believed undermined the 'level playing field' principle in competition between member states. He was also strongly in favour of an expansion of EU membership to the former Communist countries of central and eastern Europe. Above all, Major was keen to introduce the concept of subsidiarity into the text of the Maastricht treaty – thus ensuring Brussels would agree to leave it to the member state governments to decide what could best be done at their level of decision-making and what at EU level. He assured MPs that he did not intend to wreck the prospects of the Maastricht treaty but neither was he going to abandon his tough demands in order to negotiate a compromise settlement that would endanger British national interests. In the Commons vote that followed the debate, Major secured a convincing majority of 101. Perhaps more importantly, only six Conservative MPs voted against his government's pre-negotiation stance. It looked as though he had won the confidence and trust of almost all of his party over an issue that could so easily have torn them apart.

But Major harboured no illusions. He recognised that he faced the prospect of tough negotiations with his European colleagues if he hoped to secure all the points he had set down in his agenda. It was to prove an early test of his reputation for patience and calmness in negotiation. 'Understanding both the issues and the psychology of the players is the key to European Council negotiations,' noted Hogg and Hill. 'John Major possesses that rare combination of skills to a high degree. One wry ministerial victim of his technique as Chief Secretary to the Treasury described it as "offering you a toffee apple while removing your wallet". It was never more needed than in dealing with his fellow heads of government at Maastricht.'[13]

'Offering you a toffee apple while removing your wallet.'

COMMENT ON MAJOR'S
NEGOTIATING STYLE

Patten also admired the way in which Major conducted himself during those negotiations. 'Major managed the Maastricht negotiations with great skill. Those were still the days when he rather enjoyed meetings in Europe. They were a showcase for his skills – greater mastery of detail than others in the room; courteous but firm argument; a perhaps excessive belief in his ability to read body language; and a clear sense of what he wanted and what he could get.' Patten believed that his negotiations in December 1991 turned out to be 'an exemplary combination of party management and European diplomacy'.[14] Hurd was equally an admirer of Major's performance at Maastricht although he regretted – as did the Prime Minister – the use of the phrase produced by Major's press spokesman Gus O'Donnell to the media that described the outcome as 'game, set and match' for Britain. 'This did more harm than good,' admitted Hurd. 'Negotiation like tennis is about compromise. Absolute phrases can antagonise your negotiating partners abroad without convincing your critics at home.' Perhaps that remark would suggest Hurd was no tennis player. After all, the game always produces a winner. While the preparatory work carried out by British ministers had gone reasonably well, Hurd added that it was impossible to tell what would happen in Europe 'when such work moves to the great ones at the top table'. 'They tend to know less of the merits of each question and worry more about its politics,' he admitted. 'Some of these great ones I shudder to recall, have small compunction in scorning the work of their own ministers. At Maastricht one relatively new issue, the social chapter, had not been prepared in any detail. But as it turned out the Prime Minister used his good humour, his modest manner and his grasp of detail to achieve a remarkable result for us all.'[15]

What was the outcome? Major secured most of what he said he wanted. The subsidiarity principle was written into the Maastricht treaty and the long-term goal of federalism was not. The EU institutions were also not given firm executive control over law and order or foreign and defence policy. Britain even achieved an opt-out from any future plans for monetary union in a protocol to the treaty. The social chapter was also not included in the treaty. Instead a social protocol was added which Britain was able to opt out from. Agreement was also reached on EU expansion into central and eastern Europe now that the Cold War was over, something Major had wanted perhaps more than anything else. No Conservative Prime Minister had perhaps returned in such triumph from a European conference since Benjamin Disraeli, then Lord Beaconsfield, had done in 1878 after the Congress of Berlin with his 'peace with honour'. Tory sceptics might later regard Maastricht as similar in its national humiliation to Neville Chamberlain's triumph of appeasement after he met the German dictator Adolf Hitler at Munich in September 1938 but this was not the mood at the time. Only seven Conservative MPs were to express their disapproval at what Major had achieved at Maastricht by voting against the treaty in the House of Commons. *When I made a statement in the Commons on the outcome I was received with acclaim and the waving of order papers*, Major wrote in his memoirs. *It was the modern equivalent of a Roman triumph.*[16]

Of course, later events were to show just how deceptive that initially favourable reaction among Conservatives turned out to be. Major's decision to delay the necessary constitutional steps required for the Maastricht treaty's ratification until after the 1992 general election turned out to be disastrous tactical mistake. But then he had no reason at the time to suspect that he was going to face severe difficulties in getting his parliamentary party to ratify the treaty whenever that vote would take place. The decision for apparent delay was understandable. As his closest advisers reasoned: 'At the time it looked like an unnecessary complication. He would have to wait for the full and final legal versions of the treaty documents and these would not have been available until well into the New Year. He would then be very short of parliamentary time before an election. There was no hurry; other

European governments, particularly those who were subjecting the treaties to a referendum would take months to turn them into law. The Prime Minister, meanwhile, surely had his European mandate.'[17] As Major admitted himself: *The negotiations had been so well received across the House that ratification after the election appeared to present few obstacles.*[18]

The domestic problems that lay in his in-tray in November 1990 were also dealt with effectively, at least in the short term, during the 16 months of his first term as Prime Minister. The most urgent was to resolve the 'Poll Tax' issue. Heseltine had been given the thankless task of finding an alternative that would prove to be less inequitable to taxpayers and meet with the party's approval. Major argued that *nothing was ruled out and nothing ruled in* on what needed to be done. It was to take five months of intensive and detailed discussion to reach a conclusion that eventually won the Treasury's approval. There were two real possible interim alternatives for an immediate alleviation of the Poll Tax demands. The first was nicknamed 'Big Bertha'. This would have involved cutting the Poll Tax by half through the generous provision of subsidies but it was estimated such a drastic move would cost up to £18 billion in public expenditure. The alternative was to pursue what were described as 'salami' tactics, designed to reduce the Poll Tax burden in instalments. This met with more understandable Treasury approval as being less expensive a strain on public finances. In the event, Lamont was persuaded to increase VAT by 2.5 per cent in his 1991 budget in order to reduce the Poll Tax burden without weakening Treasury control. But this palliative was not to settle the problem. In late March 1991 Major faced the threat of a no confidence motion in the Commons over the future of the Poll Tax. But eventually Heseltine announced the creation of what was described as the Council Tax. By doing so he removed the immediate danger that the Poll Tax issue would damage the Conservatives in the general election.

Major also used what time he still had available before the calling of the general election to sketch out his new approach to public policy at home. This was to establish an agenda that covered all his time as Prime Minister. Major's primary intention was to transform the country's public services – not through more privatisation – but in restoring them to the high quality and committed ethical standards that he believed people should or had come to expect. Major wanted to demonstrate to the sceptical electorate that the public sector would be safe in his hands, that the Conservative Party did not despise the public services or want to destroy them. This feeling stemmed very much from the experience of his own early experiences. *My own life history was different from that of most of my predecessors at Number 10. When I was young my family had depended on public services.*[19]

Major's determination to transform the quality of the public services by raising standards and improving staff morale was genuine and heartfelt. He claimed he was not naïve or starry-eyed in this endeavour. He recalled from his own experience how inadequate the public services could be for millions of people with phones answered grudgingly if at all, long waiting times and letters and phone calls not returned. Major expressed his anger at the *lofty views of cosseted politicians, the metropolitan media or Whitehall bureaucrats* who took a cynical or amused view of what he wanted to do. While he accepted Mrs Thatcher's privatisation offensive should continue, he believed there should be limits to the advance of the free and unregulated market into areas like education and health. Major unveiled his intentions in a speech on 23 March 1991 when he used the term –'Citizen's Charter' for the first occasion. *At the time it was greeted with some disdain by a number of colleagues and commentators*, he admitted. *They failed to see its relevance and completely under-estimated my will to force it through.*[20]

Major decided not to risk calling a general election until almost the last moment in March 1992. He remained uncertain just how the voters would respond to his short period as Prime Minister. Certainly by-election results had not pointed to a Conservative victory. Moreover, the economy showed few signs of much recovery with negative growth in both 1991 and 1992, rising unemployment, a stagnant housing market and a tight squeeze on public expenditure. It was hardly a success story, even if few people in opinion polls blamed Major personally for this. In contrast a substantial majority regarded Mrs Thatcher as the main reason for the recession or international conditions that were beyond the control of any British government.

The March 1992 general election campaign was rightly to be regarded as Major's personal triumph. But the campaign itself rarely seemed likely to be so in its initial stages. The original Conservative plan was to hold a series of 'meet John Major' sessions across the country where the Prime Minister would meet people in an informal setting to answer their questions and convey a reassuring image of reason and common sense. His advisers later admitted these get-togethers were not a success.

'When the press turned up at tea time at Sawtry Village College, what they found were two or three hundred solid burghers of Huntingdon, a little drowsy after Sunday lunch. Even the typically ringing tones of Jeffrey Archer who introduced the Prime Minister at all the "Meet John Majors" could not compete with the effects of roast beef and Yorkshire pudding. The audience listened politely as the Prime Minister chatted to them, perched in their midst on his bar stool. Dubbed a "talkabout" by the *Times*, the press concluded that the whole thing was a set up, the questions all carefully planted, the audience hand picked for their docility. Once they had formed that judgement, the "Meet John Major" format was doomed for election purposes.'[21] But his set speeches in halls were not any more successful either. He could not keep to time and lost valuable live television coverage as a result while he continued to insist on endless redrafts of what he wanted to say. His whole campaign in its first few days seemed to be dogged by amateurism and disorganisation.

On the other hand, the Conservative general election manifesto was well received as Major's own personal testament. Even the irascible Norman Tebbit, still one of Mrs Thatcher's staunchest supporters, expressed his approval for the document. 'It is neither narrow nor dull,' he admitted. 'It does not depart from Thatcherite fundamentals but finds new ways of adopting them into everyday life. It is full of prudent ambition, short on slogans, full of practical ideas. Some commentators may call it dull, but if you are waiting for a council repair team or the hip operation which never seems to be on time, Major's manifesto is the most exciting for years.'[22] *It is all me. Every last word of it is me*, enthused the Prime Minister.[23]

It is all me. Every last word of it is me.
MAJOR ON THE 1992 MANIFESTO

The manifesto was inordinately long, at more than 50 pages. But perhaps the fact that it won Tebbit's backing suggests it did not give full rein to Major's proclaimed compassionate conservatism. In his signed foreword to the document the Prime Minister declared his belief in *a responsible society*.[24] This certainly meant looking after *those who cannot look after themselves*, but it also included the protection of Britain *in a dangerous world* as well as protection of both *law abiding people from crime and disorder* and the value of the currency *without which all spending pledges are worthless and all savings at risk*. Moreover, Major's view of the role of the state did not sound especially paternalistic or caring. *I believe in a society which does not try to take responsibility away from people*, he wrote. *Politicians must never make the mistake of thinking the state always knows best or that it is entitled to the lion's share of people's money. I believe in low taxes not just because they ignite enterprise — the spark of economic growth — but because they put power and choice where it belongs; in your hands.*

Major went on to declare that he did *not believe the answer to every problem is simply for government to dig deeper in your pocket.* But he also suggested that government needed to respond to the demands and aspirations of its citizens. The implementation of the Citizen's Charter was to take pride of place in his domestic agenda if the Conservatives won the general election. Major promised a *quality revolution* in the public services. This would follow the successes he said he found in the private sector as *British goods were once more winning in the toughest markets abroad. There is new vigour in the businesses liberated from state ownership; better management and better industrial relations*, he added. *These are the firm foundations of economic recovery.*

In the last paragraph of his foreword Major sought to artic- ulate a wider vision of a future under the Conservatives, of *a decent life in a civilised community. That is the way we can live; celebrating our achievements, not nurturing old grudges; enjoying our successes, not talking Britain down. We can be free of old prejudices and class bafflers [sic]. We can encourage diversity, not division; achievement not antagonism. We can all make our contribution to the success of the United Kingdom and we must keep the kingdom united. Only the best is good enough for Britain*, he proclaimed in his last banal line.

Of course, much of Major's 1992 general election manifesto was platitudinous and glib. Some of its promises turned out to be hostages to fortune. If re-elected, the Prime Minister promised his government would *make further progress* towards a basic income tax rate of 20p in the pound. The manifesto also spoke of reducing *the share of national income taken by the public sector* down from its current level of 43 per cent and promised a return to a balanced budget as the economy recovered from recession. It also declared the Conservative intention of creating a capital-owning democracy with the spread of the ownership of shares, homes, pensions and savings. The Conservatives promised to make inheritance tax less inequitable. The manifesto advocated more privatisation and deregulation, encouragement for science and innovation, and a better deal for the regions and small businesses. It devoted considerable space to how the quality of public services in the health service and in education would be achieved. The manifesto ended by placing Major himself at the centre of the Conservative campaign: 'We have a new leader, proven in office and a new agenda – yet a tried set of principles. Those principles reflect our conviction that Britain has done best when the people of Britain have been given the personal incentive to succeed. National success has not been primarily the result of accidents of geography, landscape and natural resources. Nor has it been the result of government action and state control. Success has been won when we have given our people their head; when their natural skills, talents, energy, thrift and inventiveness have been released, not suppressed. That was true when this century began; it is still true as this century draws to its close.' The manifesto was almost lyrical in its concluding, inspirational prose. 'Britain should approach the Millennium with head and spirits high, with a strong economy, with a high standard of living, with generously endowed and well managed public services and with secure defences. We want Britain to be an example to the world of how a free people can make the very best of their destiny. That prospect is within the grasp of us all. We must now make it happen.'

Of course, few voters ever see, let alone read, party election manifestos. But Major – in his old-fashioned way – gave his own party's document careful attention and he believed it was important to stake out the agenda for his own government and not merely suggest it was a continuation of Mrs Thatcher's.

In the first part of the 1992 campaign there seemed little prospect of a clear Conservative victory. Indeed, Major's efforts to make contact with the voters seemed doomed to failure. Then came the dramatic turning-point. Major complained to his team on his campaign plane as they flew back to London from Cardiff: 'Why was he not meeting any real voters? Why was he not allowed to speak to them direct? He was becoming cut off. His message was not getting across. Well he'd had enough of it. He wasn't going to sit there while his campaign collapsed around him. Why shouldn't he do what he had done all those years ago when he first started out in politics, find a street corner, get on a soap box and talk? Damn it, he was going to do it, no matter what anyone said.' Despite contrary advice from his colleagues, he did so the very next day in Luton. It was typical of the Major style of politics. Never comfortable with spin-doctoring and control freakery, he returned to the techniques used on the hustings of 30 years ago. His soap-box street meetings may not have swayed many doubting voters towards the Conservatives and they caused real headaches for the police with crowd control, but the important fact is that they transformed Major himself. 'He had come out of the crowd positively crackling with electricity. He was a different person. No more Treasury speak and whirring sub-clauses. Instead a tough street fighter who drew his strength from direct contact with a crowd and knew how to speak their language – simple, uncomplicated English spoken straight from the heart. They had found the key that unlocked the real John Major. And typically he had had it in his pocket all the time.' As his advisers admitted the soap box worked 'because it showed the Prime Minister as he was; a bit homespun maybe, but transparently honest, physically coura-geous and prepared to fight for what he believed in. At a time when all the clever talk was that electioneering in Britain was destined to draw on techniques copied from across the Atlantic, the Prime Minister went back to an older, truer British tradition. In doing so he turned conventional wisdom on its head and destroyed the whole premise on which his own campaign had been constructed.'[25]

The reasons for the Conservative victory were, of course, innumerable. The party won, in part, as a result of what Labour did. It was argued that many people feared a gov-ernment led by Neil Kinnock would bring higher taxation in an already deep recession, ensure economic incompetence and herald a return to trade union power. Shadow Chancellor John Smith's proposals to raise national insurance contribu-tions on middle income earners was also seen as a Labour own goal. And to cap it all there was the infamous Labour mass rally in Sheffield where Kinnock, in a fit of hubris, punched the air in triumph.

Major's triumph was not, however, simply the result of what turned out to be a wrong-footed Labour campaign. It owed a great deal to his own performance. The immediate consequences of such a victory were well conveyed by his advisers: 'Nothing could destroy the fact that, against the odds, the Prime Minister had pulled it off. He had done what he had longed to do since November 1990 – win his own mandate. For the first time he was his own man. He had rid himself of his inheritance and emerged from the long shadows cast by Margaret Thatcher. The Conservative Party, which could not have won without him, lay at his feet. The tensions of the last seventeen months were behind him. From now on, he could set his own course through calm waters.'

> **Neil Kinnock** (b. 1942) entered Parliament in 1970 and became Labour leader in 1983, succeeding Michael Foot. His first period as leader was taken up with struggles with the Hard Left, culminating in his defeat of the Militant Tendency at the 1985 Party Conference. He began the process of restoring the Labour Party to electability, defeating a leadership challenge from Tony Benn in 1988, but he resigned after the defeat at the 1992 general election. He served as a European Commissioner from 1995 to 2005, and was made a life peer in 2005.

Major in his memoirs admitted that the bewildering arbitrariness of the British electoral system failed to deliver him a comfortable Conservative overall majority in the House of Commons that ought to have matched the impressive size of the popular vote his party had received in the polls. *On an even national swing our lead in terms of seats would have been over seventy*, he wrote.[26] In the event, his overall parliamentary majority over all other parties was only 21. The Conservative lead of 7 per cent over the Labour party (42.8 per cent compared to 35.2 per cent of the total votes cast) may have been 'one of the biggest leads in votes since 1945 but it yielded only a miserly majority of seats'. Major did not seem particularly overjoyed at the outcome. Jonathan Hill saw the look on his face at the news of victory; 'stunned, tired and drawn'. It did not really feel like glad morning again.[27] Indeed, the Prime Minister perhaps harboured deep forebodings about the future. It seemed he was now in his prime. But he was soon to find his best of times were already over.

Chapter 4: The Beginning of the End

Major was not to enjoy much of a honeymoon period after his general election victory. Indeed, his problems began to emerge almost at once. The Prime Minister lost Chris Patten, his Party Chairman, from the government after his defeat at the hands of the Liberal Democrats in Bath. A close friend, he had provided Major with sound advice and support in the months after he became Prime Minister. Patten decided not to seek an early return to the House of Commons and instead he accepted Major's offer of becoming the last governor of Hong Kong before the colony returned to mainland China in 1997. Patten turned out to be irreplaceable. A few other Conservative Cabinet members, most notably Ian Lang, Douglas Hurd and Michael Heseltine, were willing to help Major but he was to find himself increasingly isolated. He often appeared to be a solitary and rather forlorn figure, still a believer in seeking consensus through reasoned discussion and compromise but temperamentally incapable of establishing the intellectual self-confidence and decisiveness that was necessary to be an effective Prime Minister as the pressures on him began to mount.

Within two months of victory his government was once again having to grapple with the issue of Europe because of the need for the ratification of the Maastricht treaty. Little trouble affected the early passage of the Maastricht Bill through the House of Commons where it won by a comfortable majority through a first and second reading. Only 22 Conservative MPs voted against the second reading. But then on 2 June 1992 the Danes voted unexpectedly and narrowly in a national referendum not to ratify the Treaty. They did so in a second referendum in May 1993. The Maastricht Bill was supposed to enter its committee stage in the House of Commons on the very day after the Danish referendum result. Now the whole ratification process had been thrown into serious doubt. Major decided to delay pressing ahead with the Maastricht Bill until the Danish situation had been resolved. It was a step that encouraged the Eurosceptics on the Conservative backbenches who now sought to mobilise themselves to derail the entire ratification process. In a sign of looming trouble, as many as 69 Conservative MP's signed an early day motion that called for a new approach to Europe.

But it was the financial crisis of September 1992 that intensified conflict inside the party to breaking point over the European issue. On 16 September the pound was forced out of the European ERM in humiliating circumstances. In his memoirs Major acknowledged that the events on that day which was dubbed Black Wednesday were a *political and economic calamity* for his government. *It unleashed havoc in the Conservative Party and changed the political landscape of Britain*, he admitted. *On that day a fifth Conservative election victory which always looked unlikely unless the opposition were to self-destruct became remote if not impossible.*[1] The Conservatives fell behind Labour in the opinion polls. Except for a few weeks in the autumn of 2000 – during a fuel tanker drivers' dispute – the party did not come within hailing distance of Labour again in electoral popularity until the election of David Cameron as Conservative leader in November 2005. As a result of one shattering event the Conservatives lost their popular reputation for economic competence.

Major took full responsibility for what happened on Black Wednesday. Its consequences were to rumble on through the rest of his premiership and beyond. But the economic signs were already looking gloomy before September 1992. The Treasury in the summer had forecast a further rise in open unemployment, a widening trade deficit and a growth in government borrowing. *My hopes of a growing economy to bring about a gentler Conservatism were gone*, lamented Major. *Instead to correct the economy we would have to take decisions that were bound to hurt those I most wished to help.*

It [Black Wednesday] *unleashed havoc in the Conservative Party and changed the political landscape of Britain.*

MAJOR

The turbulence on the international financial markets was not confined to Britain that autumn. Speculation brought a wave of currency devaluations across many countries in the industrialised world. But sterling was particular vulnerable with its high value inside the European Exchange Rate Mechanism. The unexpected rejection of the Maastricht treaty by the Danes added to the financial uncertainties. President Mitterand's sudden decision to hold a similar referendum in France that September made matters even worse. The result of his announcement was to push the pound down from DM 2.91 to DM 2.80 on the foreign exchange markets and perilously close to Britain's agreed ERM floor of DM 2.778. In addition, the Deutschmark continued to rise in value and this put further pressure on other currencies while the price of the American dollar fell. Major described such currency fluctuations as a *witches' brew*. His persistent attempts to convince Chancellor Kohl that he needed to deal with the over-valued Deutschmark fell on deaf ears. The Bundesbank continued to raise its discount rate.

Europe

The European rift with the Party, which Major had tried to conceal, was exposed as interest rates rose to 15 per cent in September 1992. On 16 September sterling was forced out of the ERM; the day soon became known as 'Black Wednesday'. The pound was subsequently devalued against other European currencies by at least 10 per cent. This withdrawal represented a personal defeat for Major; as membership of the ERM, the key to his economic policy, had been intended to keep inflation under control. The ensuing economic recovery during Kenneth Clarke's tenure as Chancellor did little to heal the wound over European that Black Wednesday had exposed. When Major submitted himself for re-election as Conservative leader in June 1995 it was the Europhobe John Redwood who resigned from the cabinet and challenged him, a sign that it was on the European issue that the Conservative Party was primarily divided.

The Conservatives played the Eurosceptic card in the run-up to the 1994 European elections, with Major receiving plaudits from the Conservative Europhobes by calling for a 'multi-track, multi-speed, multi-layered' Europe. The Conservatives polled just 34.7 per cent of the vote to Labour's 44.24 per cent; an indication that the electorate was tiring of Conservative infighting over Europe. In November 1994 the internecine Party conflict moved into very public centre stage. John Major took the unprecedented step of depriving eight Euro-sceptic MPs of the Party whip, resorting to the kind of strong arm tactics never before applied by a conservative prime minister no matter how irritated they had been by backbench dissent.

The Referendum party, formed in 1995 by Sir James Goldsmith, called for a referendum on the Britain's entry into the Euro. The Conservatives reluctantly adopted the same policy in the face of apparent hostility from the public towards Britain's entry. When the Labour Party followed suit, the Conservatives had been robbed of the one issue where they carried public opinion, namely that they were against the Euro, whilst the Labour Party were in favour.

As early as 28 July 1992 Major and his Chancellor Norman Lamont had discussed whether they ought to devalue sterling either inside or outside the ERM. They decided not to take such a drastic step for the moment. There was an understandable fear that doing this would not prevent a further damaging rise in British interest rates but would further undermine foreign confidence in sterling. *We had looked over the precipice and decided against jumping*, admitted Major. But the international financial situation did not improve over the August holiday period. An attempt by 18 central banks to support the American dollar failed to ensure stability. Major believed this marked *the first big victory for the markets and gave them a taste of blood that left them on the prowl, hunting ailing victims into which they could sink their fangs.*[2] Further pressure was applied unsuccessfully on the German government to cut interest rates. Major's warning that if such action was not taken other European economies would have to raise their interest rates made no impact. On 4 September the Treasury was compelled to borrow more than £7 billion to support the value of the pound on the foreign exchange markets and Lamont failed to convince the German government of the urgent need for a cut in their interest rates at a meeting of EU finance ministers in Bath.

Norman Lamont (b. 1942) was one of the so-called 'Cambridge Mafia' of Conservative politicians who had been at the University in the 1960s, all future Cabinet ministers, including Kenneth Clarke, Michael Howard and John Gummer, and was President of the Cambridge Union in 1964. First entering Parliament in 1972, as MP for Kingston upon Thames, he was Chief Secretary to the Treasury when Nigel Lawson resigned in 1989, staying in that post under his successor John Major. After his turbulent time as Chancellor, he was defeated at the 1997 election, but went to the House of Lords as Baron Lamont of Lerwick.

A financial meltdown now threatened the position of sterling. Publicly, Major tried to reassure the markets with a resolute defence of the exchange rate of the pound and support for his Chancellor in a speech to Scottish industrialists. But his intervention made no impact on events. Major refused to contemplate a devaluation of the pound in line with a similar move by the Italian lira. But now the Germans grudgingly cut interest rates by a mere quarter of one per cent. It proved to be too little and too late. Pressures continued to mount on sterling, fuelled by Bundesbank governor Professor Doctor Helmut Schlesinger who remarked publicly that tensions within the ERM were not over and that further devaluations among the European national currencies could not be excluded. His comments triggered further damaging speculation against sterling and the pound fell below its ERM floor on the New York exchanges in trading on 15 September. Dealers who bought sterling in New York were then able to make substantial profits by selling to the Bank of England at the ERM intervention rate.

The following day proved to be one of the most damaging in British financial history. Major was well aware of what might happen. *It'll be an interesting day. Stick with me and see what happens*, he told Jonathan Hill.[3] From seven o'clock that morning he remained in close touch with unfolding events. The Bank of England made the first move – by raising interest rates by 2 per cent to 11.0 per cent. This action failed to calm the markets. The Chancellor then declared publicly that the government was 'prepared to take whatever measures are necessary to maintain sterling's parity within the ERM'. But just before lunch he rushed ashen-faced to see the Prime Minister along with Robin Leigh-Pemberton the Governor of the Bank of England and his deputy Eddie George. Lamont told Major they faced choosing one of three unpalatable options – to raise interest rates still further, to realign the currency within the ERM or pull out of the ERM completely for at least a temporary period. Lamont favoured the third option but Major argued that if this was done sterling's departure from the ERM could not be only for a short time. The Prime Minister called in other senior Cabinet colleagues – Heseltine, Clarke and Hurd – to listen to their opinions on what to do at a crucial lunchtime meeting in Admiralty House. All of them were pro-European Cabinet ministers and they were reluctant to accept the Chancellor's advice to suspend membership of the ERM. Instead, they said they favoured another hike in interest rates in a further effort to calm the markets. This was done with an added 3 per cent increase taking the rates to 15 per cent. The meeting proved, however, to be inconclusive on the Chancellor's options and Major agreed to make further pleas to Germany and France for immediate action.

At 2.15 that afternoon Major phoned Chancellor Kohl and told him that unless the European central banks intervened at once to buy sterling and cut interest rates the pound would have to leave the ERM unilaterally. But the German Chancellor did not respond. In a further meeting at 4.40 p.m. with Lamont, the Prime Minister was told the new 15 per cent interest rate had failed to calm the markets. 'It is a pistol to our heads and with higher interest rates and a lower exchange it is a double disaster' admitted Clarke. Major now accepted they would have to suspend sterling's membership of the ERM. It was after this that Major informed the Queen that the government could no longer hold its position and would have to take the pound out of the ERM. He believed he would have looked like King Canute if he had tried to continue holding the line. At 7.30 that evening Lamont stood in front of the media outside the Treasury to announce Britain's suspension from ERM membership. At the same time interest rates were cut from 15 back to 12 per cent.

Major accepted that this decision represented a terrible defeat for his government. *I went to bed half convinced that my days as prime minister were drawing to a close*, he admitted. He even drew up a resignation letter. His aides and Cabinet colleagues argued against him taking such a drastic step. His sister Pat seemed to have offered decisive advice; 'You do as you think. But you shouldn't run away. You've just been elected. What about the people who voted for you? Are they asking you to go?' *The weight of pressure was to stay and not to depart*, wrote Major later. *I was never certain then that it was right nor am I now.*[4]

His official biographer Anthony Seldon summed up the Prime Minister's trauma on Black Wednesday. 'No one can know for sure the inner effect the events of September 1992 had on Major. Even the very strongest person would have found it shattering – He had acted on what he regarded as the best advice in the country and had taken what he thought were the brave and right decisions. Now he found himself widely reviled. He had never felt so lonely or exposed in his working life.'[5] Major continued to believe long afterwards that British membership of the ERM had actually made a positive impact on the economy. He argued that it helped to reduce the inflation rate and imposed some crucial financial discipline on economic management. *We were climbing out of recession* before Black Wednesday, he insisted. *We were to enjoy seven years of growth without wage or price inflation difficulties. This was unprecedented in recent years and the ERM deserves much of the credit. It hurt but it worked. The ERM was the medicine*

*to cure the ailment but it was not the ailment and no amount of
rewriting history can honestly make it so.*[6]

Major came under criticism from his Chancellor for his
behaviour on Black Wednesday after he dismissed Lamont in
March 1993 and replaced him at the Treasury with Kenneth
Clarke. In his own memoirs Lamont denied that he had
spread a rumour that the Prime Minister suffered a nervous
breakdown on that day but he did suggest Major had been
'far too calm and slow to take the difficult decisions that
we needed. He seemed unwilling to face up to the issue'.[7]
Lamont argued that during the crucial lunchtime meeting
with Major and his senior Cabinet colleagues he told them
he wanted the pound to be immediately withdrawn from the
ERM. 'We were bleeding to death and all we were doing
was talking. We had clearly lost the battle but the generals
refused to recognise it.'[8]

But Hurd as Foreign Secretary had a rather different recol-
lection. 'We were told late in the morning that every minute
of discussion cost the reserves £18bn, that every remedy had
been tried and that we should immediately suspend British
membership of the ERM. We were none of us in any position
to gainsay this advice. I argued and others agreed, that if this
was to happen our partners should be told and the rules of
the ERM followed. It could not be sensible to act in a way
which would destroy trust in all our other decisions. Failure
was one thing, panic another.'[9] As President of the Board of
Trade, Michael Heseltine blamed Lamont for indecision at
the fateful meeting. In his memoirs he remembered being
unaware of the gravity of the financial crisis until his arrival at
Admiralty House for the meeting. 'John Major and Norman
Lamont were under the most intense pressure; for me there
was no such build up,' he confessed. 'Norman presented the
background and set out what he thought to be the options

facing us. If he had said firmly that in his view there was no choice and that he could not accept responsibility as Chancellor other than to make an immediate decision to withdraw from the ERM I [and the others] could not have resisted. But that was not the way it was put to us. What we were presented with were alternatives.'[10]

Black Wednesday and the mounting Conservative parliamentary revolt over the Maastricht treaty ratification hardened attitudes in the party towards the whole European project. *Many Conservatives threw logic to one side; emotional rivers burst their banks*, wrote Major. *For a few of my parliamentary colleagues Black Wednesday awoke the instincts that turn a profound love of one's own country into a nationalism and insularity that encompasses a distaste for any other. In short, a small minority became not only pro British but anti foreign. For those like me who believed in a tolerant, pragmatic, outward looking Conservatism, the transformation was deeply disturbing.*[11]

The 1992 party conference in October found Major being forced onto the defensive. Mrs Thatcher led the assault with a claim that if Britain signed the Maastricht treaty it would mean handing over 'more power to unelected bureaucrats and would erode the freedom of ordinary men and women', while her close ally Norman Tebbit launched a brutal attack on the government's whole European policy. Major was never a wholehearted enthusiast for the European Union project. As he told the 1992 party conference: *Emotion must not govern policy. At the heart of our policy lies one objective and one only — a cold, clear-eyed calculation of the British national interest.*[12] But he was not prepared to back down in the face of party opposition over the ratification of the Maastricht treaty. As he reasoned: *I had given my word on behalf of Britain and I had done so only after having my negotiating aims overwhelmingly endorsed by parliament. Moreover Parliament had supported, indeed acclaimed the*

*deal when it was laid before it. I did not see how we could honour-
ably repudiate a treaty we had helped to negotiate. The long term
damage to our national prestige would have been appalling and it
was astonishing that there were those who could not see what to me
was quite obvious. If we acted in such a fashion who could trust
us in future? Our reputation as an honest nation would have been
lost. I was not prepared to rat on the deal I had done. This was
not a matter of pride or stubbornness. It was simply that I pledged
Britain's word. If Parliament over-ruled me – as it had the power
to do – then I do not believe I could credibly have represented Britain
again and I would have resigned.* But his determination to stand
firm over the ratification of the Maastricht treaty began to
arouse increasing hostility on the Conservative backbenches
and mutterings of discontent among some of his sceptical
Cabinet colleagues – Michael Portillo, Peter Lilley and John
Redwood whom Major in an unguarded moment in front of
a microphone was to describe as the *bastards*. The government
faced close votes in the House of Commons as the anti-Maas-
tricht forces tried to defeat ratification through a campaign of
ambushes and retreat, often voting with the Labour opposition. On 8 March 1993 Major's government lost by a majority
of 22 on a vote on the composition of a European Community
committee on the regions, with nearly 50 Conservative MP's
backing the Labour Party. But on 20 May, the Maastricht
Bill passed its third reading by a massive 180 majority as
Labour supported the government. As many as 46 Conservative MP's voted against their government on that occasion.
However, this was not to mark the end of Major's troubles. A
vote was then held in the Commons on the EU social chapter
UK opt-out from the Maastricht treaty. Major lost it by eight
votes as his party opponents backed the Labour opposition.
At once he announced there would a vote of confidence in his
government on the following day and he warned that if it was

lost he would resign. In the event, the Conservative rebels came to heel and Major won the vote with a majority of 38. The protracted saga over Maastricht ratification wearied and bewildered the Prime Minister. As he wrote in his memoirs: *Was there something I could have said, some policy I could have adopted, somebody I should have fired, someone I could have hired, a speech, a broadcast, an argument which might have begun my party's journey back to sanity? Could a different man have done it? If so, I am no closer in my mind now to answering these questions than I was when they tormented me at the time. It would be comforting to believe that there was nothing anyone could have done. If there was, the knowledge of what it might have been still eludes me.*[13]

Chapter 5: Substance without Style

It may have been understandable that the prolonged and agonising decline of Major's government through the next four and a half years after September 1992 with its endless divisions over Europe, and constant Conservative complaints over his alleged weak leadership should have dominated the public debate in the media for most of the time. But despite this, his second term in 10 Downing Street was also highly productive in domestic policy-making. Although Major's own compassionate conservatism might have lost its way in the endless series of setbacks and mistakes, the Prime Minister managed to preside over a fairly full legislative agenda between 1992 and 1997 that needs to be recalled and not under-estimated. Much of what was achieved during those years reflected many of the views and ideas that were shaped by his own personal experiences in the road from Worcester Park to Westminster. They were also to be built upon and not rejected by the New Labour project after May 1997.

The most striking was Major's approach to education policy. As he explained in his memoirs he placed education at the top of his personal agenda for government action. In doing so, he argued that he was partly following in the great Conservative tradition of Benjamin Disraeli, Arthur Balfour and R A Butler. But it also reflected his own concerns. *I had failed at school and while I could not prevent others from doing so, I could prevent the system from failing them*. Major argued that his intention was to improve the opportunities of those children who were the most deprived and excluded from society. *Bad schooling unassessed and unreformed can be overcome in homes with books but even then not easily*, he explained. *But bad schooling falls heavily on youngsters who come from homes without a single book. If the 'classless society' was to mean anything those youngsters needed a ladder to climb and the first rung had to be better education*.[1] Major recognised that better education could not be achieved overnight in the way that he wanted, that it required a long haul and would have to overcome many difficulties, not least from the teaching profession itself. But he was determined to put *excellence and choice at the centre of the education system*. Major wanted to provide nursery schools to all children *as soon as was affordable*. He favoured a return to basics in the classroom to ensure reading, writing and arithmetic were taught proficiently in primary schools. He favoured an extension of testing in all state schools and insisted that the results should be made known to parents. Extension of choice was to come through the encouragement of more grant-aided schools free from local authority control and an expansion in the assisted places scheme in public schools so that the able children of lower-income families could secure access to the best education. After 1992 comprehensive league tables of overall school performances were published annually. A National Curriculum was introduced to improve standards in primary schools. An Office of Standards in Education (Ofsted) was established by the government to supervise and implement the changes. Teacher training was also improved through the creation of a public agency. A new regime for genuinely independent inspection of schools was introduced. From 1993 technology colleges were founded – state secondary schools mainly in deprived areas and specialising in mathematics, science and technology backed by private-sector sponsorship. (They looked very much like the trust/foundation schools legislated for by New Labour in 2006.) Local educational authorities were to lose many of their powers and become more enablers than providers. Under Major there was also a dramatic expansion in higher education. What he saw as the *false divide* between universities and polytechnics was abolished.

It is true that not all of the Prime Minister's aspirations for education were carried through into solid achievements. The Treasury put up a stiff and successful rearguard action against any state funding for nursery schools. His aim had been to ensure all children under four could attend one by 1997. This failed to happen. Moreover, his radical plan for the introduction of an infant education voucher system never left the drawing board. But the Prime Minister did not deviate from his conviction of the need for educational reform in the name of parental choice and freedom. His views were to be uncannily followed by his successor Tony Blair as the New Labour project turned – with Conservative support – to a radical introduction of trust schools and a break-up of the old comprehensive school system after 2006.

In his approach to the National Health Service, Major pursued an agenda that was designed to improve the position of patients in line with his belief in the Citizen's Charter. His declared aim was *to break down the monolithic structure* that had existed in the service for 40 years. Instead, he favoured the creation of *a system of self-managing hospital trusts, encouraging though not compelling general practitioners to become fund holders, looking after their resources on behalf of their patients*.[2] The Prime Minister assured that such a radical reform would not lead to the abolition of the National Health Service, which was still guaranteed to remain 'free at the point of delivery'. In 1990, more than 200,000 patients had to wait more than 12 months for treatment; by the time he left Downing Street nearly seven years later that figure had dropped to 15,000 and most people could be expected to receive hospital treatment within six weeks. An internal regime of bench-marking, league tables and targets was also introduced in an attempt to encourage greater efficiency as well as sensitivity to the needs of patients in hospitals. Once again, there was a genuine resemblance between Major's health service policy and that of Tony Blair.

But Major was to be disappointed by the popular reaction to his Citizen's Charter approach to the public services. *It failed to catch the public imagination as it should have done with the sheer scale and breadth of its attack on old-fashioned working methods and poor public service*, he admitted. *We were so quiet about our revolution that few noticed the wall being scaled.*[3] Major accepted that what he wanted to do could not achieve an over-night success. It was a *long, slow process of change* but he believed it was here to stay. Moreover, he was convinced that under his government the public services had improved significantly. As he insisted; *School results improved; in our hospitals and doctors' surgeries more patients were treated and treated more quickly than ever before. People could tell for the first time which services were doing well and which were failing. They were able to demand better and often they got it. – The public services emerged strengthened, better funded and with more response. We peeled back the layers of complacency in the system that had led the public expecting the worst from the services their taxes paid for.*[4] The years of the New Labour

Project and Blair's agenda for public service modernisation after May 1997 owed much unacknowledged gratitude to what Major had first begun despite Labour opposition.

Major was not an obvious social liberal in his attitude to crime and punishment but again his attitudes derived from personal experience. With a tough Home Secretary in Michael Howard, he championed what at the time looked like a rigorous and punitive approach to wrong-doing. The 1994 Criminal Justice and Public Order Act removed the right of a person to remain silent on arrest and made it clear no inference should be drawn from this in court if the charged person refused to speak. Greater help was provided for the victims of crime and steps taken to speed up court procedures. A new prison building plan was started. Steps were taken to tighten up control of offensive weapons. A national crime prevention agency was established in 1995 and public money was poured into a range of measures such as the expansion of closed-circuit television cameras in areas at greatest risk of crime and a further growth in neighbourhood watch schemes. The number of police was increased and their pay improved significantly. Major emphasised the need for a firm law and order policy in a speech he made in January 1996: *Crime is not one of those trivial issues which grabs the headline for a day and is then forgotten. For all decent people it offends their sense of right and wrong. As Prime Minister my aim is to ensure we have a system of justice which protects the public and the innocent; that respects the victim; and which punishes those who break our laws.* He believed that more attention should be paid by government to society and to the complexities of the world in which real people with real problems lived. As he questioned: *How could anyone with a Brixton boyhood like mine not do so? I know very well the temptations which crowd the path of anyone whose life or prospects seem hopeless. I have seen how bad environments breed mischief and mischief breeds bad environment and how an upbringing can curse – or bless – a child for ever.*[5] Major used to argue that people could live honestly – as the majority did – no matter what their social background or level of income. He did not believe that the criminal could be either excused or forgiven because he or she was a passive victim of the evils of society. He spoke and acted from his own boyhood experiences in the inner city, not with the data compiled by focus groups, to know that the real victims of crime were the poor, the old and the downtrodden. *The greatest cruelty is to be found in tower blocks and in 'sink' estates and high density housing, hurting most whose voice is hardly heard in the making of policy. They are the unluckiest people in the community and yet crime smashes most often on their frail front doors*, he argued.[6] Again, there were similarities to Blair and his 'Respect Agenda'. But unlike Blair Major did not denounce the 'infamous Sixties' but saw that decade as important in spreading tolerance and understanding. It is true that Britain did not really become a more socially equitable society under Major. But the widening divisions in inequalities of wealth and income that emerged so dramatically during the Thatcher years at least appeared to slow down and even level off. The

Another member of the 'Cambridge Mafia', Michael Howard (b. 1941) held various ministerial jobs in successive Thatcher governments after entering Parliament in 1983. He was Secretary of State for Employment when Mrs Thatcher fell, and retained that post until becoming Home Secretary in a reshuffle in 1993. Known for the slogan 'Prison Works', there was a fall in recorded crime during his time in office. He stood unsuccessfully for the leadership after the 1997 election, and was Shadow Chancellor under Iain Duncan Smith. In 2003 he was elected Conservative leader unopposed, but resigned after defeat in the 2005 general election.

massive explosion in the wealth and power of the super-rich came under New Labour, not Major.

It was not only in his basic domestic policies that Major's government made some sensible and modest advances after 1992. As Prime Minister he also presided over one of the most substantial periods of economic recovery in Britain for nearly half a century. Of course, it is arguable whether he could claim much personal credit for this surprising and not often recognised achievement. Perhaps the predominant reason for recovery stemmed from Britain's ignominious departure from the European Exchange Rate Mechanism. It provided Norman Lamont but especially Kenneth Clarke, his able successor at the Treasury, with the freedom and flexibility to pursue an independent financial strategy. Major called his chapter on the British economy in his memoirs 'From Rags to Riches'. It certainly seemed so after the depths of recession reached during the early 1990s when open unemployment climbed to just under three million. But the price of recovery meant a rise in indirect taxation over three successive years in breach of his election promises as the demand for public borrowing soared. *Those of my colleagues who urged me to raise income taxes as well grossly under-estimated the importance of our reputation as low tax party*, wrote Major.[7] Stringent policies may have assisted in ensuring an economic revival but they also inflicted severe damage on the reputation of the Conservatives for being the party for the competent management of the economy, a negative feeling which was to last into the new century. But paradoxically during Clarke's four-year stint at the Treasury Major's government managed to stage a strong recovery. *In the last months of the Parliament the healthy economy was taken for granted as sleaze, Europe and short term dramas took centre stage*, noted Major. *It is ironic that in 1992 we had won an election in a recession and were about to lose one in a glowing economic atmosphere. Somewhere the gods must have been chuckling. The iron law of politics that a good economy leads to a good election win was about to be broken.* In his memoirs, he set out the achievement succinctly: *As I left office the figures told the story of the fall and rise of the economy. On the day I became prime minister the tax burden was 36.3 per cent. On 1 May 1997 it was 36.6 per cent which over the span puts our tax record in a proper perspective. During my premiership interest rates fell from 14 per cent to 6 per cent; unemployment was at 1.75 million when I took office and at 1.6 million and falling upon my departure; and the government's annual borrowing rose from £0.5 billion to nearly £46 billion at its peak before falling to £1 billion. The economy was growing by only around 0.5 per cent in 1990, shrinking by 1.5 per cent in 1991 before recovering to grow by 3.5 per cent in 1997. During the depths of the recession I inherited, all the economic indicators worsened but they had all been corrected by May 1997. Above all, we had broken the inflationary psychology that had so bedevilled our economy. In November 1990, the rate of inflation was 9.7 per cent. In May 1997 it was 2.6 per cent. It was a fine legacy.*[8]

It is ironic that in 1992 we had won an election in a recession and were about to lose one in a glowing economic atmosphere.

MAJOR

In industrial and employment policies Major followed the Thatcherite agenda quite closely. This was most apparent in further privatisations. The most controversial concerned the break-up of the railway network as it was moved from state control and into private ownership. The Prime Minister took a rather romantic view of railways, based on childhood memories of steam engines and the logos of the old operating companies before nationalisation. *I want to remove British Rail for good from the stand-up comedian's joke book and turn it into the envy of the world*, he promised in January 1995.[9] The resulting deliberate fragmentation of the network with the separation of the ownership and management of the infrastructure from train operations looked the worst option for change even at the time when it was being carried through. The shattered outcome by 1997 was 18 passenger franchises, three rolling stock companies, five freight businesses, six infrastructure services and 15 central service businesses. The whole maze was supervised by two sets of regulators while the government was still required to take overall responsibility for the railway network. His sympathetic biographer Anthony Seldon suggested that 'rail was the borderline privatisation of the Major government and that it was proceeded with at all was a sign that Major could override unease in the House of Commons and bureaucratic inertia despite unfavourable circumstances'.[10] It is perhaps significant that Major omitted to mention the rail privatisation decision anywhere in his 774-page autobiography. It turned out to be an unmitigated disaster.

The other substantial privatisation of the Major years was less contentious though highly symbolic. The coal industry had been nationalised by the first post-war Labour government in 1946. This honoured a long-held commitment to the miners. But by 1992 the coal industry faced an uncertain future. The miners had been crushed by the 1984–5 strike and pit closures and redundancies accelerated as productivity improved and the market for coal contracted. Soon after the disaster of Black Wednesday the Prime Minister was nearly overwhelmed by a sudden and unexpected crisis that hit the mining industry. On the eve of the party conference, Heseltine suddenly announced that British Coal intended to close down 31 pits and make 30,000 miners redundant. It was to be the most savage contraction of the industry since the great strike eight years earlier. The announcement unleashed storms of protest not only across the Labour Movement but among some on the Conservative backbenches who regard the closure plan as a betrayal of the Nottinghamshire miners who had worked defiantly through the 1984–5 stoppage and in doing so helped to ensure the defeat of the NUM president Arthur Scargill. Major admitted it had been wrong to declare an immediate contraction of the workforce. *I recognised from the moment the storm broke that we would have to execute a swift and undignified partial U turn*, he wrote.[11] But he refused to back down completely on a decision which the Cabinet had not even discussed. Instead further taxpayer's money was ploughed into the coal industry to ease the pain and ensure more training and better redundancy arrangements for the miners. It was also agreed that each pit closure would be determined by an independent review panel to judge on the lack of its commercial viability. Heseltine took most of the blame for the public-relations fiasco but the whole sorry affair aroused further disturbing doubts about the Prime Minister's own competence and what appeared to be his dithering style of leadership. Major's professed belief in a caring Conservatism that was concerned with the benefit of ordinary people seemed oddly out of tune with the pit closure announcement. Only six Conservative backbenchers voted against the government over the issue and a further five abstained. But opinion surveys found that Major had become the most unpopular Prime Minister since Sir Anthony Eden in the aftermath of the Suez crisis in 1956. Four years later the coal industry was privatised with hardly a murmur even from the remaining miners.

Major was less successful in privatising the Royal Mail and the Post Office. There was a lack of Cabinet agreement on what to do. Both Chancellor Clarke and Heseltine wanted a radical privatisation of the service. But *in the end the Royal Mail proved to be one of those areas where because of doubts within the parliamentary party we were not able to reach satisfactory solutions*, Major admitted.[12] The main opposition came from a group of right-wing Conservative MP's who took a nostalgic view of the Post Office. But even Major's own policy unit fell short of recommending the complete transfer of the Post Office to the private sector. Instead it was decided to try and encourage more competition through a loosening of the restrictions holding back its commercial development. Many in the Cabinet were concerned about how old age pensioners would respond to such a change and they realised they faced the threat of effective industrial resistance from the still powerful Communication Workers union. The way in which the Post Office problem was handled was seen as yet further embarrassing evidence of a failure of prime ministerial political nerve. The *Sunday Times* denounced Major as a 'man of straw'.

The Prime Minister also presided over the continuation of a more pro-active labour market strategy, which had first started in the autumn of 1986 under Lord Young as Employment Secretary to encourage the jobless back into paid work. The integration of the state owned Job Centres with the payment of unemployment benefit to claimants through technological investment in new computer systems and the introduction of the 'availability for work' test speeded up the process of job placement. The introduction of the Jobseekers' Allowance demanded that nobody could refuse genuine work opportunities on offer and remain in receipt of benefit. Family credits were also introduced to help people to move themselves off welfare and into paid work. Measures were also taken by Major to improve training and skills. In 1991 the Training and Enterprise Councils were created. They were described somewhat extravagantly as 'the most significant peacetime partnership between government and industry this century'.[13]

Labour trends began to improve. After January 1993 the level of unemployment began to fall month by month. Strikes almost disappeared from the scene. Unit labour costs showed some signs of containment while productivity began to look better in comparative international league tables. But there was not much sign of Major's One Nation Toryism in his attitude to the trade unions and forms of tripartism between labour, capital and the state. While he may have sounded more emollient and readier than Mrs Thatcher to meet delegations of trade union leaders and listen to what they had to say, he was not prepared to offer them any concessions on substantial issues or a new kind of social partnership, similar to those of every other country in western Europe. Major had no wish to bring back the days of so-called beer and sandwiches to 10 Downing Street with a more conciliatory approach to the Labour Movement. Indeed, in 1992 he abolished the tripartite National Economic Development Council and its secretariat, first established by Harold Macmillan nearly 30 years earlier. In his opinion trade unions had no obvious role to play any longer in policy making and he believed they should confine their purpose to helping employers improve productivity and reduce their labour costs. The 1997 Conservative general election manifesto promised further regulation to limit the right of employees to call industrial action in the 'essential' services. Major would not restore the right to trade union membership for staff at the government's communications headquarters in Cheltenham that had been taken away from them by Mrs Thatcher in 1984. Nor did he display much interest in a concerted government policy to improve the position of the low paid. In 1993 he abolished the country's statutory Wages Councils which had sought to provide a safety net for those working in poverty in specific unorganised sectors of the labour market ever since their introduction by the then Liberal President of the Board of Trade Winston Churchill in 1908. Major remained opposed to the idea of a national statutory minimum wage. It was hard to find much sign of a progressive government agenda on employment matters during the Major years. The Prime Minister argued that Britain needed to create a more flexible labour market through deregulation and a neo-liberal agenda that would encourage individualism and enterprise. In this, his approach looked similar to that of New Labour after a batch of early legislation after 1997 designed to shift the balance of power a little away from employers and towards employees.

The 1997 Conservative general election manifesto gave robust expression to the free market cause. It claimed that under Major during the 1990s the spread of the free market had been one of his government's greatest triumphs. The manifesto spoke of pushing forward still further 'the economic revolution' that Mrs Thatcher had begun in 1979. The Conservatives contrasted the dynamic British model with its emphasis on flexibility and enterprise with what it saw as continental Europe's 'failing social model'. Such language was uncannily similar to that used by Blair and his Chancellor Gordon Brown after they came into government in May 1997.

Chapter 6: Facing Ethnic Nationalism

John Major was served by two able men at the Foreign Office – Douglas Hurd up until May 1995 and then Malcolm Rifkind for his last two years. But he was also keen as Prime Minister to make an impact himself on international relations. His calm and effective handling of the first Gulf War in 1991 suggested that he was quite capable of shaping a distinctive and responsible foreign policy. Unfortunately for him, the troubled world beyond Britain was to cause him considerable anguish during his second term as Prime Minister. The most difficult of all those foreign problems was the bitter civil war that brought about the break-up of Yugoslavia between 1992 and 1996. Perhaps the biggest mistake in British government policy towards the Balkans took place as early as August 1992. Major was presented then with a detailed assessment of what armed preventive intervention might mean to Britain by the military chiefs of staff. It provided him with sober reading. They suggested as many as 400,000 troops, three times the current size of the British army, would be required to bring an end to the bloodshed and separate the combatants. Moreover that massive force would need to stay in former Yugoslavia for many years to come. Major accepted this sombre analysis without much apparent questioning. *It was inconceivable that anything could be done without full-scale NATO involvement and that was not forthcoming*, he argued in his memoirs. *Other countries too, no doubt, had made the same bleak military assessment.*[1] But perhaps as a result there was no apparent appetite in the Cabinet in the late summer of 1992 for any substantial military intervention in Yugoslavia. Major believed the best that could really be done was to try and somehow minimise the level of civilian casualties and set a limit to the area of the conflict and prevent its spread across the entire region. It was therefore decided to send a token contingent of 1,800 British soldiers to protect food convoys that were organised to supply the growing number of refugees with the basic means of life. Even that decision aroused some Cabinet opposition. But Major insisted that this was the least they could do. He feared that doing nothing at all would not bring peace to south-eastern Europe and at least helping to protect food supplies would help to prevent mass starvation as over a million Bosnians faced the prospect of death from cold and hunger in the coming winter.

In November 1992 the contingent of British troops arrived on the ground to carry out their mercy mission. But it soon became clear that this was not nearly enough and the military presence would need to be expanded as the conflict grew more savage, especially around the Bosnian capital of Sarajevo. The crucial question was whether an intervention by the forces of western Europe could or should be made to enforce a peace in Croatia and Bosnia, even if this meant having to wage war against the combatants and in particular on Slobodan Milosevic's Serbia which had launched an aggressive campaign of ethnic cleansing, aimed especially at Bosnian Muslims in a determined strategy of territorial expansion. Former British Foreign Secretary David Owen and former US Secretary of State Cyrus Vance suggested in their joint efforts to broker a peace suggested that Bosnia needed to be broken up into ethnic-based cantons but such a suggestion proved to be unacceptable to all the interested parties to the conflict. Bill Clinton's newly elected American administration wanted to lift the arms embargo that had been imposed on the region and to launch air strikes against the Bosnian Serb positions around Sarajevo as a way to force Milosevic and his allies to the negotiating table. But Major rejected such an idea out of hand. He put it down to an *element of campaign rhetoric* by Clinton.[2] The Prime Minister even feared that President Clinton's apparent determination to act decisively in the Balkans threatened to provoke *the most serious Anglo-American disagreement since the 1956 Suez crisis*. Apparently the Americans were not prepared to make any military commitment themselves that would have involved placing their own troops on the ground in the region. Instead they said they wanted to pursue a so-called 'lift and strike' strategy even though this would have endangered Europe's supposedly neutral position towards the conflict, disrupted vital relief operations and put British and other European forces at risk. Major's military advisers were against both lifting the arms embargo on the Muslims and air strikes against the Serb forces in Bosnia. The Prime Minister was also worried about the Bosnian threat of reprisals against British troops if he acted in such a way. But this remained a difficult position to defend publicly. It meant that his government and those of other European countries were, in effect, telling the Muslims of Bosnia – sorry, we cannot lift our embargo on your access to arms so you can match the substantial hardware, especially artillery, being deployed by the Serbs in their siege of your towns. Major acknowledged his stance placed Bosnia at a serious tactical disadvantage unless its people were prepared to roll over and accept the brutal occupation of their country by the Serbs with the resulting probable massacre of their population. In retrospect Hurd admitted the policy had been a strategic mistake. It had enabled the Serbs to persist with their murderous assaults on unarmed Bosnian civilians. Even after the massacre of 68 people in Sarajevo market on 5 February 1994 Major could not get his own Cabinet to agree on an ultimatum to the Serbs to withdraw their heavy guns from the hills surrounding the Bosnian capital. The Major/Hurd strategy was not only inglorious but ultimately hopeless as it helped to prolong the tragedy and the terrible ethnic cleansing, atrocities not seen in Europe since the Second World War.

Perhaps too many people in high places shared the attitude of a senior diplomat who told this author at a Ditchley Park conference in early 1993 that the most sensible move would be for NATO to create a *cordon sanitaire* around the countries of former Yugoslavia and leave their peoples to kill each other off. The insouciance and *de haut en bas* attitude of too many at the Foreign Office was the decisive factor. The non-intervention policy in the Balkans at that time looked eerily similar to the official British attitude to the Spanish Civil War nearly 60 years earlier when the Republicans were left to their fate and the Fascist powers openly backed General Franco's forces with men and armaments.

The bloody stalemate in Bosnia and Croatia was to continue until October 1995 when peace talks eventually opened between the combatants at Dayton, Ohio under the auspices of an activist President Clinton. Major remained unrepentant in his memoirs about his government's general attitude. *Many countries did nothing to help the people of Bosnia. Britain was not one of them*, he argued. *I feel there was no alternative policy which would have been better than the one we followed. Had there been an alternative policy at any stage which was within our power and would have saved more lives I would have taken it.*[3] It was, in fact, only when the Clinton administration decided to act strongly that the terrible conflict was brought to an end. The efforts of Britain and the rest of the European Union had proved to be limited, modest and ultimately futile. They tended to prolong rather than bring an end to the horrors. Major admitted that there were simply never enough United Nations or NATO forces deployed to make much of a difference. The unilateral imposition of a settlement on the warring parties by force of external arms was simply regarded as an impossibility for far too long. In fact, it might have been better either not to have intervened at all from the beginning or to have imposed an early settlement that recognised the independence of the new states that had decided to break away from Yugoslavia. Later events in Kosovo when NATO air strikes brought an end to Serb aggression against the Albanians suggested that a more robust military strategy in 1992–3 might have ended the tragedy of Bosnia much earlier.

The Balkan wars were to add to the difficulties that Major was to experience with President Clinton. The Prime Minister had enjoyed a close personal friendship with his predecessor in the White House, George Bush. He had even appeared to allow the search of Home Office files for information on the young Clinton's time as a student at Oxford University in the late 1960s for the

Had there been an alternative policy at any stage which was within our power and would have saved more lives I would have taken it.

MAJOR

Republican Party to use against Bush's opponent in the 1992 presidential election. But Major had to work with Clinton for four-and-a-half years in the so-called special relationship between their two countries. It was hardly a match made in heaven. 'In their see-saw relationship there was rarely a cross word when they talked together; the difficulties always arose when they were apart', wrote Anthony Seldon.[4]

The two men met for the first time in February 1993 in Washington soon after Clinton's inauguration. It was outwardly cordial enough, even if they seemed to have differences of view over both Bosnia and Ireland. Like so many British prime ministers before him since the end of the Second World War Major was keen to encourage and develop the so-called special relationship. For his part, Clinton seemed less enthusiastic. Initially the Prime Minister admired Clinton's political skills but he believed the President was too preoccupied with his domestic popularity to take any risks abroad. *At times in the early days of his presidency I found him alarmingly under-briefed*, he recalled. *But when he turned his attention to an issue he would immerse himself completely in it.*[5]

It was Northern Ireland that was to colour their relations for much of the time. Major inherited the province's intractable troubles in November 1990. It was a part of the United Kingdom of which he knew very little. *My previous political offices had not prepared me for the subject and the conventional wisdom was that prime ministers were well advised to keep their distance*, he later recalled.[6] His first awareness of the IRA came soon after he took office. On Thursday 7 February

Forty-second President of the United States, William Jefferson Clinton (b. 1946) had served five terms as Governor of Arkansas before becoming the Democratic contender against George Bush Snr. in 1992, despite allegations about his personal life. He was re-elected in 1996, the first Democrat to serve two full terms since Franklin Roosevelt. Despite campaigning largely on domestic issues ('It's the economy, stupid'), his presidency saw major initiatives to resolve the Arab-Israeli conflict, as well as in Northern Ireland and the Balkans. Surviving impeachment over a sex scandal in 1999, he stood down in 2001, his Vice-President Al Gore having lost the election to George Bush Jnr.

1991 they fired three mortars from a stolen van parked in Whitehall at 10 Downing Street in the middle of a Cabinet meeting. Nobody was injured but it was a narrow escape. It did not seem like a propitious introduction to a problem that had perplexed successive British prime ministers for nearly a quarter of a century. But Major was not content to pursue a containment policy towards Northern Ireland. Instead, he decided to try and make some progress and break free from the impasse that had often intimidated his predecessors. Major possessed no master plan for Ireland in his back pocket but he believed in the politics of reason and thought he needed to get to know the people and problems of Northern Ireland. In his memoirs he pointed out that he visited the province more often during his time as Prime Minister than any other part of the United Kingdom. Major devoted his formidable negotiating skills in an attempt to make some progress even if the chances of achieving a breakthrough and some kind of peace settlement seemed remote.

His lack of historical knowledge about Ireland was probably an asset rather than a liability for Major in the beginning. It meant he was not over-awed by the often-restricting burdens of history that had paralysed so many attempts at securing peace in Northern Ireland. But a number of important decisions were made in his early months in 10 Downing Street that helped to create a more constructive climate. Peter Brooke, his first Northern Ireland Secretary, was impatient to try and break the deadlock. At his suggestion Major agreed to make it clear that Britain had 'no selfish, strategic or economic interest in Northern Ireland' and there was no intention 'to occupy, oppress or exploit' the province. Such a public declaration made a positive impact on Sinn Fein/IRA leaders Gerry Adams and Martin McGuinness even though it made explicit what had become a strong assumption of British government policy for many years. What Major also explained, however, was that his government had no intention of over-riding the democratic wishes of the majority in the province who wished to remain inside the United Kingdom. Although his government would not stand in the way if a clear majority of people in the Province expressed a wish to end the partition of Ireland, nor would it try to force the majority into accepting reunification.

Major was encouraged into believing a peace process might make some headway in Northern Ireland after he received a surprisingly positive message from the IRA leadership in February 1993. What influenced his assessment of how to respond were the words that the IRA used in their confidential statement to him. The terrorist organisation now asserted; 'The conflict is over but we need your advice on how to bring it to a close.' The message added that the IRA wished to announce a 'cease-fire in order to hold a dialogue leading to peace'. Major was sceptical at first about this approach and he was well aware that many of his Cabinet colleagues sensed the IRA was seeking to trap the government and remained insincere in its efforts. The IRA terror bombing attack on 20 March 1993 against Warrington shopping centre in which two young boys – Tim Parry and Jonathan Ball – were murdered and a further 56 people injured seemed to confirm the view that the organisation's leadership was less than sincere in seeking help in initiating a peace process. Just over a month later the IRA carried out a bomb attack on Bishopsgate in the City of London with one dead and 47 injured. In addition, a brutal IRA sectarian bombing in a fish-and-chip shop in the Protestant heartland of the Shankill road in Belfast added to the strains.

Throughout this period of bomb outrages and murders by the IRA Major continued to hold informal talks with Sinn

Fein, the terrorist organisation's political arm. He made it clear in his memoirs that he was keen to emphasise to the Sinn Fein/IRA leadership that his government did not intend to lean on the Unionist community to accept any moves towards an end of Ireland's partition. Adams and McGuinness might have hoped Major and his colleagues would act as 'persuaders' of the Protestant majority in Northern Ireland in bringing about reunification. *The idea was unrealistic and undemocratic*, insisted Major. While he was open minded about any possible way of reaching a settlement in Northern Ireland, the Prime Minister insisted there could be no constitutional change in the position of the province within the United Kingdom without the clear consent of a majority of its people. This assurance had been turned into a constitutional guarantee by the post-war Labour government in 1949. Major – like all his predecessors since that year – argued that *the democratic right of self-determination* must remain with the people of Northern Ireland. There was no possibility whatsoever that a British government would try and bring about change in the province over the heads of its elected politicians. The Prime Minister found too much of his time was spent trying to convince the Irish government of Albert Reynolds as well as the Clinton administration in Washington that they could not afford to ignore or sweep aside the Unionist parties who were firmly opposed to any moves that might lead to the end of partition.

In the aftermath of the IRA outrages in Warrington and the City of London Major made it clear that no positive move could be expected by his government towards Sinn Fein until the terrorist organisation not only called a cease-fire but announced it would ensure a permanent end to its campaign of violence. He suggested that an initial period of ten weeks of peace would be proof that the IRA were sincere in their declared wish to move away from terrorism. In the murky world of military intelligence and secret assignations, understandable suspicions were aroused among many Unionists that Major and his government intended to reach a settlement with IRA/Sinn Fein at their expense. The tortuous exchanges between London, Dublin and Belfast were leaked and added to Unionist anxieties that the Prime Minister was behaving in a duplicitous way and intent on negotiating a rapid deal with the terrorist organisations. McGuinness leaked some of the information on the talks and declared publicly that Major was ready to accept only proof of a two-week IRA cease-fire before starting negotiations on a settlement that would bring about an eventual united Ireland. *This self-interested piece of Republican propaganda was a tissue of lies*, insisted Major in his memoirs.

But the Prime Minister was in his element in the seemingly endless round of parallel negotiations he held during much of 1993 with Sinn Fein/IRA and the Reynolds government in Dublin. On 15 December a joint declaration was finally reached between the British and Irish governments that sought to encourage the launch of meaningful negotiations. Its eventual production owed much to Major's patience and attention to detail. His diplomatic skills were most in evidence in the success he achieved in winning the reluctant support of Unionist party leader Jim Molyneaux for what he wanted. Major was also adroit in ensuring that nothing would appear in the joint declaration that would encourage anybody to believe that there was a secret agenda that would lead through a process of compromise to Ireland's reunification. The Prime Minister was keen to emphasise that the Downing Street declaration was *a statement of principles and not a deal negotiated with the paramilitaries of either side*. Major later insisted that it was *a powerful symbol* that showed the way forward after nearly a quarter of a century of almost perpetual conflict. He admitted that the joint declaration was often written in language that was *convoluted and dense* but he argued that this was because the negotiators had wanted to establish a painful balance. As Major explained: *Through the thicket it guaranteed fair play. Unionists were assured a united Ireland would not be imposed upon them. Nationalists were assured their traditions and aspirations would be respected. The paramilitaries were assured that they could enter political life if they accepted the rules of law and democracy and abandoned violence. The Declaration was not designed as a blueprint for a settlement but it paved the way.*[7]

But months of prevarication and uncertainty followed. Gerry Adams demanded a 'clarification' of the joint declaration. The Sinn Fein leader was strengthened in his attitude by President Clinton's decision – against the advice of many of his own officials – to grant Adams a visa to travel to the United States for Easter celebrations in 1994. The readiness of the White House to provide the Sinn Fein leader with such an entry incensed Major, especially as Adams proceeded to denounce the British government during his stay in Washington. However, on 31 August came the breakthrough. In a statement the IRA announced a 'complete cessation of military operations' in response to what the organisation called 'the potential of the current situation and in order to enhance the democratic process'.[8] They added that their decision underlined their 'definitive commitment to its success'. The IRA also agreed that the joint Downing Street declaration provided 'an opportunity to secure a just and lasting settlement' of the Northern Ireland problem although a solution would be possibly only 'as a result of inclusive negotiations'. In his response, Major welcomed the statement but he said wanted to see the IRA's conciliatory words reflected in its actual deeds on the ground. He disclosed in his memoirs that British intelligence believed the IRA was still keeping the option of a return to terrorism open. The statement had failed to provide an unequivocal assurance that the cease-fire would turn into a permanent cessation of violence. Nonetheless, Major proceeded to announce some confidence-building measures as a sign of his own sincerity and based on the debatable assumption that the IRA did indeed intend to abandoned its terror campaign for good. On 21 October 1994 he announced that an exploratory dialogue would begin with all the parties by the end of the year. But in his memoirs Major acknowledged that the Ulster Unionists were right to remain doubtful about the IRA's intentions. Intelligence told him that the organisation was *taking advantage of the cease-fire to recruit new volunteers and at times openly to reconnoitre targets.* As he admitted: *As ever we did not have the luxury of taking a one-sided view. A settlement could not be achieved just by pandering to the IRA.*[9]

However, on 9 December 1994 British officials and Sinn Fein leaders met together publicly for the first time in over a quarter of a century. Highly complex and inter-related negotiations now continued through the early months of 1995 at various levels in the search for an agreement. It was always hard going and the dangers of a complete breakdown and a return to violence were always apparent. Major presided over three strands of negotiation. The first was aimed at establishing a new form of internal self-government for Northern Ireland. The second looked at how future relations between the two parts of Ireland were to develop and the third involved discussions on the future of Anglo-Irish relations. *All three strands had to interlock*, explained Major. *No assembly for the Unionists without north/south institutions for the Nationalists; no Dublin involvement for the Nationalists without an amendment of the 1937 Irish Constitution* [to remove its territorial claim to represent Northern Ireland] *for the Unionists. The mantra of the talks remained; 'Nothing is agreed until everything is agreed'*.[10]

The months that followed the calling of the IRA cease-fire brought little substantial progress. As time ebbed away the position of the Unionist leader Jim Molyneaux became increasingly untenable as a growing number of his party members feared that the British government was caving in to the pressure coming both from the Republican movement and the Irish Prime Minister over the formation of cross-border institutions that they believed would lock Northern Ireland into an irreversible process that would lead to eventual Irish reunification. Constant denials of this by Major and his colleagues failed to convince the Unionists. In August 1995 Molyneaux felt compelled to resign from the Unionist party leadership. He was replaced by David Trimble who was at first seen as a hardline Orangeman after his recent appearance complete with sash on the march at Drumcree. The Prime Minister later admitted he had not concentrated enough on the fine print and draft texts of the complex negotiations and had spent too much of his time and energy in bringing about the ceasefires. He was fortunate that Trimble turned out to be more compromising and realistic than initially seemed likely to be the case.

The real obstacle to progress, however, lay in the IRA's willingness or otherwise to give up its arsenal of weapons. The Downing Street declaration had made it clear there would have to be a 'permanent end to the use of or support for paramilitary violence' and a commitment to 'exclusively peaceful methods' for any meaningful negotiation about the future of Northern Ireland. But for months Sinn Fein negotiators prevaricated on this crucial issue. One moment they insisted demilitarisation would require the removal of all British troops from Northern Ireland and the disbanding of the Royal Ulster Constabulary, the next they suggested what was being asked of the IRA was tantamount to unconditional surrender. Major found himself under constant pressure from the Irish government to make unilateral concessions to Sinn Fein under the threat that if this was not done the IRA would return to its terror campaign. This was hardly a reassuring attitude if the organisation expected its professed commitment to peace to be taken seriously. Major decided to form an independent international commission under the former American senator George Mitchell to supervise the decommissioning of terrorist arms but the IRA initially expressed hostility to this. The Prime Minister envisaged that the rundown of weaponry, subject to international inspection, should go hand in hand with negotiations on a constitutional settlement. But by December 1995 the outlook appeared uncertain. Major briefed President Clinton on a visit to London that the IRA seemed ready to resume its terrorist campaign and he emphasised its direct role in punishment beatings and sectarian violence. As he explained: *As far as the IRA was concerned, not killing people for a while was the only concession they were prepared to make. They had not moved in any other respect since the cease-fire but had used the opportunities it provided to recruit, to train and to reconnoitre targets, even measuring mortar positions around Belfast's Aldergrove airport and sitting cheekily outside army barracks timing the electric gates.*[11]

George Mitchell's commission published its first report on 24 January 1996. It was seen as providing a possible way out of the deadlock. The commission suggested there was a 'clear commitment' among the paramilitaries 'to work constructively to achieve full and verifiable decommissioning as part of the process of all-party negotiations'. Mitchell was later to admit to Major that this statement had been made 'for tactical reasons' because he feared the IRA was about to end its cease-fire. In fact, the intelligence services proved to be more accurate in their information. On 9 February the IRA announced the cease-fire was over. An hour after saying this publicly they detonated a lorry packed with explosives in London's Canary Wharf complex which killed two people and injured more than 100 others. Major was told that the planning for the outrage had taken over three months, which aroused serious doubts about the IRA's professed commitment to the peace process. Despite his personal despair and revulsion at what had happened Major kept his nerve and did not abandon his negotiating efforts although there was pressure on him to do from some Cabinet ministers and Conservative backbenchers. On 28 February the British and Irish governments announced jointly that they intended to start all-party talks on the future of Northern Ireland by 10 June after elections had been held in the province in the previous month. All parties to the proposed talks would have to commit themselves publicly to the renunciation of violence. Sinn Fein participated in the election that summer and won 15 per cent of the vote, the best result they had ever achieved in Northern Ireland. But then two weeks later the IRA blew up the Arndale shopping centre in Manchester on a Saturday, injuring around 200 people, Further ritual Republican violence followed against the annual Orange Order march at Drumcree. It seemed that the province was returning to the hopeless cycle of violence that had scarred its history over the previous quarter of a century.

Major admitted in his memoirs that his work to find an elusive settlement in Northern Ireland turned out to be *the most difficult, frustrating and from 1993 the most time-consuming problem of government during my premiership.* But he said he never regretted what he had done. Certainly the problems he faced stretched his negotiating abilities to display calm, patience and restraint to the very limit. *Persuading each side to give an inch was the hardest negotiating task I have ever faced*, he wrote. *Each move had to be weighed and balanced minutely. The suspicions of each other and the British government were intense. So were the emotions. If one side was happy, I knew I had probably got it wrong. If my proposals attracted no more than grumbling and grudging acquiescence from both sides, I was perhaps on the right track.* Although Major was unable to accomplish a breakthrough in Northern Ireland, he was responsible for some significant progress. It was a sign of his maturity of judgement that he recognised – perhaps from his earlier immersion in the subject – that the Northern Ireland question was not susceptible to any final or clear-cut solution.

What advance that was made under Major represented a small tentative step along a long and winding road. The problem has too long and bitter a history, Major recognised. Attitudes and fears are too deeply ingrained. Sectarianism will take a very long time to erode. But he was surely right to believe that Northern Ireland would not go back to what it had been like in the bloody years of the 1970s and 1980s. The habits of peace, the desire for a return to the rule of law and civilised behaviour between people would eventually take root in what was a divided, traumatised and hate-filled society. But there could be no grandiose peace settlement, only a slow and often painful process of incremental steps forward. Major admitted in 1999: *The people of Northern Ireland have seen that there is an alternative to the mute acceptance of endless cycles of 'troubles' and terrorism. Attitudes to violence have changed. There is less willingness to tolerate or endorse the destructive and mindless behaviour of the para-militaries; more healthy anger against them. Whatever setbacks there may be, I do not believe that the clock can now be turned back fully.*[12]

Chapter 7: The Road to Oblivion

If Northern Ireland showed Major at his best, it did little to improve his government's overall standing with the British electorate. Sleaze was to become a byword that was inextricably linked to Major's government from the autumn of 1992 and it helped to destroy whatever remaining political credibility it still enjoyed after Black Wednesday. The seemingly endless exposure of the sexual antics and financial misdeeds of Conservative ministers and backbench MPs *fed the public belief that the Conservative Party as an institution had been in government for too long and had got into bad habits. As the mood music to the final act, sleaze chimed with the times.* Major said he took a *puritanical view of financial misbehaviour and a tolerant view of personal misdemeanours. I sought to judge every allegation by reference to two points; whether it was true and whether it constituted an abuse of public office. Nothing else, so far as I was concerned, was relevant.*[1] Perhaps it was just as well he adopted such a tolerant view of his party in the light of later lurid revelations from his parliamentary colleague Edwina Currie who revealed her role as Major's mistress in her malicious diaries. But Major was right to regard the personal antics of a handful of Conservative ministers and MP's as irrelevant to the overall conduct of his government. *The Conservative Party did not invent sin or sex but it suffered from a great appetite to uncover – in some cases almost to initiate and to encourage – scandals about personal morality*. Major spent many of his weekends waiting in trepidation for the latest revelations in one of the Sunday tabloids about Conservative colleagues. His hatred of the media grew understandably more intense as a result. *I expected the climate to turn and in a normal political cycle it would have done so*, he wrote. *But with the Conservative Party mortally wounded over Europe, our blood was in the water and the media sharks circled until polling day*. The litany of Conservative culprits and victims involved in sexual antics became seemingly relentless – David Mellor, Tim Yeo, Stephen Milligan, Piers Merchant and others.

Nor was his government free from allegations of financial corruption. One minister – Jonathan Aitken – was eventually sent to prison for perjury. Michael Mates, a junior minister at the Northern Ireland Office, may have unlawfully helped a businessman Asil Nadir in his affairs when a Conservative backbencher. Major said Mates' support had been a *misjudgement* and *not a hanging offence* but Mates then recklessly dined with a Nadir aide at the Reform Club after Nadir himself had fled to Northern Cyprus to avoid facing trial in Britain. Mates was then forced to resign. Two other ministers – Tim Smith and Neil Hamilton – were accused of having accepted money and gifts from the owner of Harrods, Mohammed Al Fayed, when they were backbenchers in the 1980s. There were also accusations of a scandal over the selling of arms to Iraq in contravention of a government embargo and the action taken by the government against a small British firm Matrix Churchill. It was alleged to have acted illegally. Major established a public inquiry under Sir Richard Scott to investigate the accusations. The resulting report cleared

The Conservative Party did not invent sin or sex but it suffered from a great appetite to uncover – in some cases almost to initiate and to encourage – scandals about personal morality.

MAJOR

the government of unlawful behaviour but Major came only one vote short of defeat in a parliamentary division after the matter was debated in the House of Commons. Critics argued that Major was too weak and indecisive in his handling of the scandals and took too naïve and trusting an attitude of his more worldly colleagues. He appointed a committee under Lord Nolan to examine standards in public life and the relationship between elected politicians and business. But when Major decided to allow a free vote on some of the Nolan recommendations he was attacked by some Conservative MP's who accused the committee of impugning their integrity.

Major became increasingly convinced that he and his government were becoming the targets of a ruthless and orchestrated mass media campaign to undermine his authority and that of his government. Understandably he was suspicious of Rupert Murdoch's News International media group, especially after it decided to work with the New Labour spin machine operated by Alistair Campbell and Peter Mandelson. But as scandals and corruption later engulfed the Blair government amidst the hubris and arrogance of its third term in government after 2005 the innumerable follies of the Major years perhaps came into better perspective.

This was no consolation for Major who often seemed distracted and obsessed by the increasingly hostile treatment he was receiving from many tabloid newspapers. His emotional hysteria over the media coverage unsettled Cabinet colleagues like Douglas Hurd and Michael Heseltine who could not understand why he treated such material so seriously. Senior civil servants were also bewildered and annoyed by the amount of their time they needed to spend on dealing with media gossip, rumour and innuendo. One told Professor Peter Hennessy that the hallmark of the Major government was 'the bunker mentality and short termism'. 'It is quite extraordinary the degree to which the PM reacts to what's in the *Daily Mail* or the *Daily Telegraph*. On Prime Minister's question days, private offices across Whitehall scan them with particular attention because if their department is mentioned, as like as not, it will be rung-up by the Number 10 private office asking for a brief in case the Prime Minister is asked about it.'[2]

But the continual assaults on his leadership and government fuelled Major's underlying feelings of resentment and insecurity. Some of his colleagues who disagreed with him over Europe and other matters also attacked him personally. John Redwood's former political adviser Hywel Williams described Major's style as 'irresolution punctuated by stubbornness'. 'This reflected the Prime Minister's own character,' he argued. 'Personality was always a more important fact about John Major than policy. He began his premiership advertising his intention to create a classless society but sensitivity about class, education and intelligence remained his hallmark.'[3]

Increasingly Major found himself bereft of trusted followers whom he could confide in. The absence of Patten from the centre of his government was a real weakness. Patten's views of his friend had been reassuring. 'Major is a clever man, much cleverer than he thinks, much cleverer than others assume can possibly be the case of someone touched by so little formal education. The lack of much by way of secondary education, and nothing by way of university education had not made Major less clever, only less confident about his intellectual authority and social skills. He was sensitive about patronising criticism and sufficiently self-knowing or understanding that he should not be. A thicker skin, a bit more ruthlessness and the willingness to trade on the tough background from which he had shot to political stardom would together have made him a happier man and probably a more successful prime minister.' Patten was impressed by what he saw as Major's 'strength of character', which was 'the more remarkable, given how easily hurt he can be and how socially vulnerable he is'.[4]

Douglas Hurd became a close confidant of the Prime Minister, especially in the difficult years after 1992. But he was struck by how much Major suffered from corrosive self-doubts as he complained continually about his political enemies 'or the fates in general'. 'Some took this as proof of his inadequacy. Rather as I learned it was a technique, a mechanism of management by means of overflow,' Hurd explained. 'Behind the parade of complaints I learned to recognise an essential integrity and confidence in his own ability to handle matters.' But Hurd also revealed that Major was 'easily upset by small personal stories, particularly if they affected his family as well as himself. He used to telephone me at seven in the morning about some tawdry piece in a tabloid which I had not read and would probably never have read if he had not rung.'[5] No doubt other Cabinet colleagues were bombarded with Major's feelings about the unfair way that he believed he was continually being treated. The tragedy was that the more he railed against the arrows of misfortune in volcanic outbursts of self-pity, the more his political enemies were confirmed in their belief that he was weak and ineffective. Surprisingly, Major failed to recruit a hard-bitten ex-journalist or a tough operator from the Civil Service like Mrs Thatcher's Bernard Ingham to manage and manipulate 10 Downing Street's relations with the media. Instead he relied on career civil servants like Chris Meyer and Gus O'Donnell to explain his policies and decisions to correspondents and they did not regard themselves as spin-doctors. In his scurrilous memoirs Meyer provided a vivid vignette of Major prowling up and down his Downing Street bedroom in his pyjamas fulminating at something he had read in the *Daily Mail* or the *Sun*. Some journalists treated the Prime Minister in public with damaging contempt. The most culpable was Alistair Campbell when political editor of the short-lived *Today* newspaper and before he joined Blair's New Labour team in 1994. Peter Oborne, the *Spectator*'s political editor, saw Campbell as the playground bully who sought to destroy Major by open ridicule and abuse. In print Campbell called the Prime Minister 'a second rate, shallow, lying little toad of a man' and likened him once to a 'piece of lettuce'. On one foreign trip when Major came down the plane to talk to journalists Campbell told him to 'sod off' because he was doing his expenses. Oborne believed 'The conversion of the Tory Prime Minister into a ludicrous comic cuts figure was probably the greatest of all the services that Campbell did for Labour'.[6]

> **Tony Blair** (b. 1953), became Shadow Home Secretary in 1992 under the then Labour leader John Smith, where he did much to change the party's 'soft on crime' image. When Smith died suddenly in 1994, Blair succeeded him and continued the work of reforming the Labour Party. He coined the term 'New Labour' and in 1995 engineering the symbolic ditching of Clause IV, the Labour Party's commitment to nationalisation of industries. This reformation of the party, together with a highly-efficient electioneering organisation, helped Labour secure a landslide victory in the general election of May 1997. (See *Blair* by Mick Temple, in this series.)

By the early summer of 1995 Major was reaching the end of his tether with the endless pressure inside the party over European issues. *The economy was coming out of recession, unemployment was falling and the public services improving. We were helping to bring peace in Bosnia and Northern Ireland. The public finances were on the mend. Taxes would soon begin to fall. Interest rates and inflation were low. The opposition had no distinct alternative to offer. Yet Labour was winning twice the support of the government in opinion polls and our position was dire.*[7] By June 1995 Major's net parliamentary majority had fallen from 21 at the 1992 general election to only ten, as the Conservatives lost a succession of by-elections with huge swings against them. After a particularly raucous meeting with Conservative backbenchers in the eurosceptic Fresh Start group, Major decided to pre-empt any move to challenge his position in the autumn that he believed was being plotted. *It is time to put up or shut up*, he declared. John Redwood, his Eurosceptic Welsh Secretary, resigned from the Cabinet to challenge Major in the battle for the leadership. In the event, the Prime Minister won the votes of 218 of his Conservative backbenchers but Redwood secured 89 while a further eight abstained and 12 more spoilt their ballot papers. It was hardly a convincing victory and Major's vote fell only three votes above of the minimum he had set himself in order to remain in the premiership. He later described the result as *less than I had hoped for but more than I had feared.* Jonathan Hill, who had returned to assist, was taken aback by Major's reaction to his win. Apparently he had the same look on his face as on election night in 1992 – 'stunned, tired and drawn. He didn't smile. He could hardly speak'.[8] His re-election did not really settle very much either. Major believed it *ended the frenzy in the party but not the conflict.* He convinced himself that at least his drastic challenge to the Conservative MPs had postponed an irrevocable split inside the party over the European issue and this was some achievement. But he also admitted that the issue was *too deep seated to be cut off at its source.*[9]

It is time to put up or shut up.

MAJOR

The final outcome for Major and his government never seemed to be in any doubt. On 17 March 1997 Major had an audience with the Queen and asked for the dissolution of Parliament. On his return to Downing Street he declared: *People are looking for change. But we are the change and we will carry forward what we have been doing for the past eighteen years. I believe this election is winnable. I think we are going to win.*[10] He tried desperately to energise his campaign by returning to his soap box in Luton but this approach no longer worked and he reverted to the relative security of his battle bus. At times Major seemed to be fighting apart from his own party as he made personal pleas to the voters to trust him on Europe, pensions and health. 'Why not?' commented one aide. 'The party is unelectable.'[11] The Conservative campaign staggered along with further revelations of personal sleaze and bloodletting over Europe right up to polling day. Major tried initially to avoid a position that meant ruling out the suggestion Britain would never join a single European currency under any circumstances. He wanted to adopt the sensible stance of *negotiate and then decide*. Many Conservative parliamentary candidates disagreed with such a cautious approach and expressed implacable opposition to British membership of any proposed euro currency in their own election manifestos. While Cabinet ministers like Michael Howard and Peter Lilley stretched their loyalty to breaking-point on the issue, the junior ministers John Horam and James Paice actually broke ranks and said they would not accept a European common currency on principle. Major was too weak to discipline them or anybody else. *Whether you agree with me or disagree with me, like me or loath me, don't bind my hands when I am negotiating on behalf of the British people*, he urged.[12] His own personal position on the euro and Europe was by no means either incoherent or unrealistic. Major could see no sensible reason in the national interest why any British Prime Minister should throw away the country's negotiating position by closing the door at that stage to any possible future entry into a European monetary union even if he had already reached a personal view that he did not favour replacing the pound with the euro. Perhaps the looming presence of European enthusiasts Clarke, Hurd and Heseltine at the heart of his government made it impossible for him to take a more resolute position. In the campaign Major accepted that *the single currency is the single most important decision that any government has been asked to make for generations* and yet he was unable to give a decisive lead on the key question of what he would do about it if the Conservatives were re-elected. But only three Conservative candidates made pro-European statements in their manifestos – Sir Edward Heath, Hugh Dykes and Ian Taylor. As many as 190 of the Conservative contenders announced in their own election addresses that they were opposed in principle to Britain joining the European common currency. Eventu-ally under intolerable pressure Major was forced to concede that he would allow a free vote among Conservative MPs on whether Britain should abandon the pound or not. It

'It is doubtful if the Conservatives could have done much in the campaign to alter the final outcome.'

DAVID BUTLER & DENIS KAVANAGH

was an inglorious moment. But by then it was becoming unclear just what he genuinely believed about Europe himself. On one occasion he even declared *If you are not prepared to be isolated in Europe, you have no right to lead your country.*

In earlier times Major could have made much of the economic successes of his government in his appeal to the electorate. However, the famous Bill Clinton maxim –'it's the economy, stupid' – made surprisingly little impact on the British voters in 1997. And yet as the Nuffield College study of the election pointed out 'for the first time since the 1950s a government could face the polls with an economic success story to tell'.[13]

In fact, the dismal result turned out to be the worst electoral disaster in the history of the Conservatives. There was a 10 per cent swing away from the party to Labour, a shift in voter preferences not seen since Labour's landslide triumph in 1945. As David Butler and Denis Kavanagh concluded in their election analysis: 'It is doubtful if the Conservatives could have done much in the campaign to alter the final outcome.' In truth, Major's government had never staged any real recovery after Black Wednesday. The 1993 and 1994 tax rises destroyed the Conservative reputation for being the tax cutting party and it had meant abandoning key election pledges. The constant revelations of financial and sexual sleaze – both serious and trivial – over the years also took their toll. Peter Mandelson, New Labour's spin-doctor gave another compelling reason for Major's defeat. 'There was no reason left not to trust New labour. All the old "ifs", "buts" and "maybes" had gone. We removed the target.' But he added: 'Without New Labour the Conservatives could have won again.'[14] That assertion looked implausible. Major's own campaign staff saw the writing on the wall from the beginning. With a lack of clear focus, the Conservatives 'had no message or at least not one that the voters listened to. Labour did'.[15] Perhaps the main cause of Major's humiliating defeat was a growing conviction among many voters that the Conservatives had simply been in government for far too long and had grown arrogant and complacent. They were also seen as exhausted, lacking in new ideas and above all deeply divided. Many Conservatives in the years before 1997 behaved as if they wanted to indulge themselves in a collective act of self-destruction.

Part Three

THE LEGACY

Chapter 8: Major – the Audit

In the perspective provided by the years of New Labour government since May 1997, John Major's record as Prime Minister looked much better than his many critics liked to suggest. He himself pointed to a significant achievement that was often overlooked by his critics. Writing in 1999 Major argued: *Labour has left the Tory legacy largely undisturbed; our trade union legislation lies in place for the moment; not one of the many privatisations Labour consistently fought in opposition has been reversed; the government has retained, in a new guise, the devolved system of management we brought to the national health service; it has delighted in exploiting the performance targets and league tables the Citizen's Charter brought to public services; it has stuck to Michael Howard's determined approach to law and order; it has even retained the tax cuts of the Tory years. Perhaps when the legacy one leaves, the successes one achieved, remain essentially intact and are protected, imitated – even built upon – by one's successors, one should take it as a compliment (whatever political abuse accompanies it) and pay tribute to the good sense of those who have cherished their political inheritance in deed if not in word.*[1]

It was Major as Prime Minister who helped to enable the creation of the formidable New Labour project. His unexpected general election victory in March 1992 had compelled the Labour Party to modernise itself still further as it realised it still needed to do much more to make itself broadly acceptable to the British voters if it hoped to be elected back into government again. What it was required to do was to accept most of the Thatcherite settlement. His shrewd political friend Ian Lang, who served as Scottish Secretary and later at the Department of Trade and Industry explained; 'Where Margaret Thatcher established a new political paradigm, John Major consolidated it. But for his years in power, much of what she had achieved might have been undone. Yet it was by taming the trade unions that she made New Labour possible; and it was his period of consolidation that gave Labour the time to become credible – a credibility founded on our policies, better presented than we could do but with presentation replacing principle.'[2]

Perhaps when the legacy one leaves, the successes one achieved, remain essentially intact and are protected, imitated – even built upon – by one's successors, one should take it as a compliment.

MAJOR

No dramatic rupture was, in fact, to occur in May 1997 with Labour's return to power after 18 years in the political wilderness. There was to be no sudden arrival of a new and radical centre-left government, comparable to those that reformed the country in 1906 and 1945. Major's crushing defeat and that of his party could not disguise the fact that there was much more continuity than change as New Labour replaced the Conservatives. Indeed, as time went by under Blair's premiership increasingly uncanny parallels appeared with the Major government. The New Labour sleaze – from David Blunkett to Peter Mandelson, from John Prescott to the Tessa Jowell/David Mills affair, from Bernie Ecclestone and Formula One to the peerages for party loans scandal orchestrated by the Prime Minister himself – suggested Blair and his government, despite his claims to the contrary, were not whiter than white as he had once promised they would be. Moreover on a very wide range of policies – from the privatisation of public services and industries to private finance initiatives, from the creation of foundation hospitals and trust schools, from countless measures to tackle crime to a prudent approach to income and wealth distribution, from the increasing use of market mechanisms for the administration of the public services to means testing and coercion for the socially excluded – New Labour mostly followed the Major/Thatcher agenda. Where Blair benefited was from having much more professional public relations and a far glossier packaging of his government's presentations, a more highly centralised and tightly disciplined control of his party and the persistent manipulation and abuse of a mostly servile media. But these were more often superficial differences of appearance and not of real substance. Even on the contentious European question, Blair seemed to grow much closer to Major's final position by 2006. Despite his promise to make Britain an influential and effective partner in the shaping of the future European Union, Blair did not take the pound back into the European Exchange Rate Mechanism or accept joining the common currency while his Chancellor Gordon Brown was hardly less sceptical than Norman Lamont in his negative attitude to Brussels, which reflected a traditional sceptical Treasury attitude to European issues. The American economic neo-liberal market model was far more admired by the New Labour project, as it was by Major, than Europe's social model.

Major's own personal contribution to the achievements of his government was to remain debatable. Every Prime Minister must respond to what the historian H A L Fisher once called 'the contingent and the unforeseen'. Their strength of character, personality traits and the extent of their intellectual abilities are usually tested to the full by how they handle events and not through careful planning or conscious design. Few Prime Ministers have found themselves fortunate enough, except perhaps for Blair in recent political history, to enjoy a prolonged absence of pressure on their room for political manoeuvre and with it the existence of invaluable public space in which to develop and implement their programmes in government. Major found few genuine opportunities available for him to demonstrate the authentic quality of what he believed to be his progressive Conservatism and to act upon it with a government record that might have resonated among the unlucky and deprived people he claimed he wanted to identify with. Anthony Seldon, his authorised biographer, argued that what Major lacked was both the time and a strong parliamentary majority behind him to give practical expression to what he wanted to do. He argued that Major 'wished to help the underprivileged and dispossessed, not least in the inner cities' and in his later speeches he pointed out that Major spoke movingly of his 'deep concern to help ordinary people which his party's high command treated with either amused tolerance or irritation but rarely comprehension'.[3] There is more than a grain of truth in this observation. As the Conservative backbencher Gyles Brandreth recalled in a diary entry: 'The party is profoundly divided, our economic policy is discredited, we are on the brink of being dragged into a Balkan War and the Prime Minister talked about the Citizen's Charter! Of course he believes in it passionately, believes it will change the life of ordinary people. Inevitably though we must all have thought it, not one of us dared say "No one gives a toss about the Citizen's Charter Prime Minister".'[4]

Moreover, Major lacked the eloquence and the persistence that were always necessary to turn his well-intentioned aspirations into a practical reality. His strangely articulated and limited vision often – in the eyes of his bewildered party – appeared to rise no higher than a call on the need for the provision of more toilets and fewer safety cones on motorways. But his Citizen's Charter was a genuinely important initiative and it sought to address serious and important questions even if many Conservatives ridiculed what he wanted to achieve. And yet sadly too often it led not to popular measures that were understandable to appreciative people who used the hospitals when ill and sent their children to state schools but instead to a veritable pandemic of managerial techniques – internal market competition, sub-contracting and inevitable bureaucracy and paper filling. 'Back to Basics' was not only an unattractive slogan but it became an excuse for the launch of sweeping and insensitive technocratic offensives that required the hiring of more and more managers and seemed to confuse and irritate the long-suffering public. There were only limited sightings of the measures needed to stimulate that opportunity and classless society Major claimed that he longed to encourage. The foundation of the National Lottery was very much his idea but it seemed to appeal to the very acquisitiveness that Major said he wanted to temper with a more compassionate attitude towards the socially excluded.

Too often exhausted and isolated, he seemed content on too many occasions merely to advance the Thatcherite agenda in government still further but without much inner conviction or energetic application. It was the lack of any coherent and practical vision of a One Nation Conservatism that could be transformed into executive action that really weakened Major. His nostalgic and well-meaning aspirations never proved to be nearly enough. As a result, he often seemed bereft of any firm purpose in government. Instead his approach was too *ad hoc*, fragmented and piecemeal. Major looked committed to a rather disjointed *à la carte* menu that lacked much intellectual coherence. He was always responding to events and not seizing the initiative or setting the agenda for government.

Major was to be the last Conservative Prime Minister in what historians called the Conservative century. After its terrible defeat the party fell into its longest and most protracted period in the political wilderness since the mid-19th century. Major should not have been turned into the scapegoat for the failure of the William Hague–Ian Duncan Smith–Michael Howard led Conservative Party that followed him between 1997 and 2005.

And yet he was to suffer from withering criticism from former Cabinet colleagues for his record as Prime Minister. In his resignation speech on 9 June 1993 his former Chancellor Norman Lamont had complained that the Major government was 'far too short termist and paid too much attention to pollsters and party managers. Too many important decisions were made for thirty-six hours' publicity'. 'Unless this approach is changed the government will not survive', warned Lamont. 'We give the impression of being in office but not in power.'[5] His carefully crafted words were deeply wounding but they were seen by his party enemies as an epitaph for his government. Lord Ashcroft, Conservative billionaire fundraiser and former Party Treasurer, was equally dismissive. 'I felt that Major was weak and indecisive and he was prone to bitching and moaning about other people, including senior figures in the party,' he wrote in his memoirs. 'Major lacked the vigour that was needed to lead the party successfully.' But Ashcroft added: 'When many years later it was disclosed that he had pursued a lengthy affair with Edwina Currie, the former Tory junior minister, I frankly thought more of him

'We don't want a leader who is ordinary. We want a leader who is extraordinary – and ... JM isn't that.'

GYLES BRANDRETH

than I had ever done before – perhaps he had more energy than I had given him credit for.'[6]

Major's real faults proved to be that he was too decent, too friendly, too kind, too considerate to others in a party that often regarded such attributes as personal weaknesses and faults of character. Brandreth caught his real problem as Prime Minister in his diaries. As he wrote in an entry on 28 September 1992 after attending a lunch with the Prime Minister alongside fellow backbenchers: 'He's down; feels it, shows it. There's no bounce. He may be letting us see this deliberately, to remind us that he's human, to take us into his confidence, to make us realise he's just like us. But we don't want to be led by someone who's just like us. We don't want a leader who is ordinary. We want a leader who is extraordinary – and decent, determined, disciplined, convincing as he is, JM isn't that.'[7]

But would either of his defeated rivals in the 1990 contest – Douglas Hurd or Michael Heseltine – have really proved any more successful than he was in leading a faction-ridden Conservative Party for six and a half years as Prime Minister? It seems doubtful. In a private minute sent to Major in May 1993 Hurd provided him with some advice on how he might improve the way he ran his government. By doing so Hurd pointed to some real problems about Major's personal style as Prime Minister. He argued that while there was 'a case for a hands-off Prime Minister like Callaghan, concerned with the outlines, not the detail. I doubt if we shall ever see such a Prime Minister again but I do not believe the Prime Minister should handle as much detail as you do. If like yourself the Prime Minister is determined to master detail then the present machinery is plainly inadequate.'

'You are better than any recent Prime Minister at question and answer,' reassured Hurd. 'This advantage must be fully maintained and exploited. But it does not provide the emphatic and authoritative aspect of leadership. It seems to me that without sacrificing anything or taking a false position, you could identify, say once a month, a Prime Ministerial occasion where you set out what you intend.' As he concluded: 'I am in favour of breaking the pernicious stranglehold of the lobby on policy presentation. They are not a good filter for your views.'[8]

But Major could not become the kind of prime minister that Hurd wanted him to be. In a masterly summation of Major, Matthew Parris perhaps understood more than anybody else what made Major the man he was. In an essay that he broadcast for the *Today* radio programme on 26 May 1997 shortly after Major's resignation, Parris declared: 'It is the fate of those who form a bridge between eras to be distrusted by those unwilling to cross and disregarded by those who make the crossing. It is the fate of those who hold the line between two equally dangerous and opposite extremes to be called indecisive from both fringes. But it is they who form the bridge; they who hold the line – who are the decisive ones. It is they who are brave.'[9]

In his often painfully honest and rather endearing, well-written and revealing memoirs Major seemed to regard himself as ultimately a disappointment as Prime Minister, mainly because he believed he was never able to explain adequately enough to the country what he stood for and what he wanted to do. Of course, he inherited a disastrous political legacy with a Conservative Party in turmoil. Miraculously he led it to a general election victory against all the odds. He went on to preside over one of the longest, uninterrupted periods in Britain of economic revival and prosperity during the 20th century that established the solid foundations for most of New Labour's own achievements after May 1997. Parris once described Major as 'a pretty, quirky individual, a maverick in accountant's clothes'. He was certainly a peculiar man to be leading the Conservative Party as Prime Minister towards the close of the 20th century. His success and ultimately his tragedy revealed a great deal about the nature of contemporary politics and the kind of country Britain had become. There might have been no Majorism, no distinctive pattern or clear narrative to his years in 10 Downing Street. Both his predecessor and successor saw themselves as messianic leaders (one even hubristically as God's servant on Earth) Unlike him they were conviction politicians who liked to lead imperiously from the front and sought to stamp their authoritarian personalities on their times. Major was utterly different. He was quieter, modest, insecure, uncertain of himself, prone to self-pity and despair and yet decent, civilised and perhaps incorruptible, not seduced by the trappings of power and the endless yearning for great wealth and high social status. He was to be constantly under-estimated.

Major would have been better advised to embrace the modernisation process and turn it into a Conservative virtue. After all, most of the trends of the next ten years were already visible in what often looked like uncoordinated fragments during his premiership. His Deputy Prime Minister Heseltine realised the need for the party and the country to come to terms with the forces of globalisation and technological change. In his competitiveness agenda at the Board of Trade he began to grapple in a bold way with what could have been a new beginning for the Conservatives. In November 1996 the government published a White Paper on free trade and foreign policy. It set out an agenda for more liberalisation in world trade and a new global role for the British economy. The document emphasised the country's position as the world's second largest outward investor and the world's fifth largest trading nation. It spoke of the dynamic City of London and its strategic strength in the making of the new global order. In June 1996 the government published its third competitiveness White Paper and the strides made to transform the economy into a successfully entrepreneurial world player. Major himself gave voice to this increasingly important theme in a speech he made in June 1996. *Our aim is to make this country the unrivalled enterprise centre of Europe with an open, flexible and dynamic economy, able to win in world markets, one that keeps social costs down for business so that prosperity can rise for all; one which promotes incentives and rewards success.*[10] Tragically for Major and his party it was New Labour and not them who became identified with this new cutting edge world of modernity. Here was the essence of a grand narrative but Major failed to focus his attention closely enough on its importance.

There were also personal failings that cost Major dear. As leader of the Conservative Party he lacked one important attribute that his predecessor had enjoyed. As Gyles Brandreth explained in his diary: 'Later I was telling Peter Tapsell [Conservative MP] about the PM's time in the tea room and he said, "Yes, he's an attractive man, intelligent and well-intentioned but he doesn't frighten anybody, does he? When Margaret came into the tea room the teacups rattled".'[11] A civil servant told Peter Hennessy; 'I like my Prime Ministers to be a bit inhumane. The PM has insufficient inhumanity. It's a government of chums. He wants to be liked. He cares deeply what the papers say about him'.[12]

Major did not seek or want to govern by fear. He was not an autocrat. He always sought to build a consensus before making a decision. But there was one important section of informed opinion that took a surprisingly complimentary view of the way he conducted his government. Senior civil servants – good judges of men – were almost universal admirers of the Major style in government and the way he ran his Cabinets. He liked to work with them and they liked to work with him. He treated the Whitehall mandarins with respect and admiration. The warm feelings were reciprocated in full.

As Prime Minister Major did not seem like a man for his times. And yet he was much more interesting and complex than his innumerable detractors were ever really prepared to recognise. It is hard not to avoid the bleak conclusion, however, that at the end of the day Major became yet another victim of the ubiquitous British class system. There was nobody ever quite like him before who rose so high to lead the Conservative Party. The slights and sneers, the jokes and innuendo about him from his supposedly better-educated and higher-class colleagues were always apparent and he understandably resented them, even if he acknowledged proudly that he was not a blue chip or a public school product, that he had not created or run a business of his own or made a personal fortune for himself at the Bar or in the City of London. As Robert Cranborne – from the grand family of Lord Salisbury and Hatfield House – once explained so insensitively in 1999: 'There was this odd mixture of misery and the limpet {about Major} – the miserable limpet if you like – which was a great inhibition to his premiership.'[13] In 2005, after eight years of abject failure and three hopeless party leaders, the Conservatives turned to a young Oxford graduate and old Etonian for their salvation. The mass media, who seemed to know little history beyond the headlines of the day before yesterday, regarded

'There was this odd mixture of misery and the limpet {about Major} – the miserable limpet if you like – which was a great inhibition to his premiership.'

ROBERT CRANBORNE

David Cameron's early efforts in bringing the Conservatives back into the political centre as a cynical sign that he sought to inherit Blair's mantle and his meretricious New Labour project by emulating it. It might have been more accurate to suggest Cameron was returning – with a patrician style of insouciance and *noblesse oblige* all of his own – to the gentler, decent, understated politics of John Major. But he did so with the important addition of a shrewder awareness of the imperatives of personality politics and use of manipulation that has become so crucial for the achievement of political and personal success in a world without ideology and notions of left and right, any sense of history and an endless obsession with modernity. Britain's most extraordinary Conservative Prime Minister bequeathed an important legacy to his party and his country to build upon. One day both may yet come to recognise and appreciate it.

NOTES

Chapter 1: An Extraordinary Ordinary Man

1. Andrew Wheatcroft, *The Strange Death of Tory England* (Penguin, Allen Lane, London: 2005) p 185.
2. John Major, *The Autobiography* (HarperCollins, London: 1999) p 726, hereafter Major.
3. Major, p 201.
4. Major, p 202.
5. Major, p 14.
6. Major, p 16.
7. Major, p 20.
8. Major, p 25.
9. Major, p 31.
10. Major, p 70.
11. Major, p 81.
12. Nigel Lawson, *The View From Number 11* (Bantam Press, London: 1992) p 710.
13. Margaret Thatcher, *The Downing Street Years* (Jonathan Cape, London: 1993) p 422.
14. Major, pp 84–5.
15. Lawson, *The View From Number 11*, p 711.
16. Lawson, *The View From Number 11*, p 712.
17. Major, p 112.
18. Douglas Hurd, *Memoirs* (Little Brown, London: 2003) p 365.
19. Major, p 113.
20. Major, p 114.
21. Major, p 187.
22. Thatcher, *The Downing Street Years*, p 850.

23. Major, p 190.

Chapter 2: Son of Thatcher or a Funny Old Tory?

1. Thatcher, *The Downing Street Years*, p 831–2.
2. Nicholas Ridley, *My Style of Government; The Thatcher Years* (Fontana, London: 1992) p 401.
3. Major, p 193.
4. Major, p 205.
5. Chris Patten, *Not Quite The Diplomat* (Penguin, Allen Lane, London: 2005) p 77.
6. Ian Gilmour, *Whatever Happened To The Tories* (Fourth Estate, London: 1997) p 349.
7. Edwina Currie, *Diaries 1987–1992* (Time Warner, London: 2002) p 247.
8. Sarah Hogg and Jonathan Hill, *Too Close To Call; Power and Politics – John Major in No 10* (Warner Books, London: 1995) pp 86–8.
9. Major, p 204.
10. Major, p 70.
11. Major, p 300.
12. Currie, *Diaries*, p 163.
13. Anthony Seldon, *Major: A Political Life* (Weidenfeld & Nicolson, London: 1997) p 370.
14. Major, p 544.
15. Matthew Parris, *Chance Witness; An Outsider's Life in Politics* (Penguin, London: 2002) p 407.
16. Patten, *Not Quite the Diplomat*, p 77.

Chapter 3: In the Prime of Political Life

1. Hurd, *Memoirs*, p 413.
2. Penny Junor, *John Major – From Brixton to Downing Street* (Penguin, London: 1993) p 209.
3. Major, p 210.

4. Major, p 206.

5. Major, p 215.

6. Major, p 233.

7. Major, p 240.

8. Major, p 243.

9. Major, p 202.

10. Major, p 269.

11. Hogg and Hill, *Too Close To Call*, p 82.

12. Major, p 265.

13. Hogg and Hill, *Too Close To Call*, p 146.

14. Patten, *Not Quite the Diplomat*, p 23.

15. Hurd, *Memoirs*, p 421.

16. Major, p 288.

17. Hogg and Hill, *Too Close To Call*, p 161.

18. Major, p 346.

19. Major, p 246.

20. Major, p 252.

21. Hogg and Hill, *Too Close To Call*, p 209.

22. Hogg and Hill, *Too Close To Call*, p 220.

23. *Conservative General Election Manifestos* (Routledge, Politico's, London: 2000) pp 355–418.

24. Hogg and Hill, *Too Close To Call*, p 225.

25. Hogg and Hill, *Too Close To Call*, p 263.

26. Major, p 307.

27. Hogg and Hill, *Too Close To Call*, p 259.

Chapter 4: The Beginning of the End

1. Major, p 312.

2. Major, p 318.

3. Major, p 330.

4. Seldon, *Major*, p 323.

5. Major, p 341.

6. Norman Lamont, *In Office* (Warner Books, London: 1999) p 250.
7. Lamont, *In Office*, p 251.
8. Hurd, *Memoirs*, p 426.
9. Michael Heseltine, *Life In The Jungle* (Coronet, London: 2000) p 340.
10. Major, p 352.
11. Major, p 363.
12. Major, p 371.
13. Major, p 385.

Chapter 5: Substance without Style

1. Major, p 394.
2. Major, p 392.
3. Major, p 261.
4. Major, p 262.
5. Major, p 387.
6. Major, p 388.
7. Major, p.677.
8. Major, p 689.
9. Quoted in Wolmar, p 72.
10. Seldon, *Major*, p 502.
11. Major, p 670.
12. Major, p 667.
13. *Conservative Party General Election Manifestos* (London: 2000) p 419.

Chapter 6: Facing Ethnic Nationalism

1. Major, p 535.
2. Major, p 539.
3. Major, p 548.
4. Seldon, *Major*, p 353.
5. Major, p 499.

6. Major, p 446.
7. Major, p 455.
8. Major, p 458.
9. Major, p 461.
10. Major, pp 463–4.
11. Major, p 485.
12. Major, p 492.

Chapter 7: The Road To Oblivion
1. Major, p 550.
2. Peter Hennessy, *The Prime Minister: the Office and its Holders since 1945* (Penguin, London: 2000) p 474.
3. Hywel Williams, *Guilty Men* (London: 1998) p 31.
4. Patten, *Not Quite the Diplomat*, pp 78–9.
5. Hurd, Memoirs, p 415.
6. Peter Oborne, *Alastair Campbell, New Labour and The Rise of the Media Class* (Aurum, London: 1999) p 101.
7. Major, p 609.
8. Hogg and Hill, *Too Close To Call*, p 283.
9. Major, p 646.
10. Major, p 698.
11. Major, p 699.
12. Major, p 715.
13. David Butler and Denis Kavanagh, *The General Election of 1997* (Macmillan, London: 1997) p 230.
14. Major, p 716.
15. Butler and Kavanagh, *The General Election of 1997*, p 232.

Chapter 8: Major – The Audit
1. Major, p 734.
2. Ian Lang, *Those Blue Remembered Years* (Politico's, London: 2002) p 310.

3. Seldon, *Major*, p 744.
4. Gyles Brandreth, *Breaking The Code* (Weidenfeld & Nicolson, London: 1999) p 120.
5. Lamont, *In Office*, p 382.
6. Michael Ashcroft, *Dirty Politics Dirty Times* (MAA Publishing, London: 2005) p 57.
7. Brandreth, *Breaking the Code*, p 120.
8. Hurd, *Memoirs*, p 509.
9. Parris, *Chance Witness*, pp 415–16
10. *Conservative Campaign Guide* 1997, p 51.
11. Parris, *Chance Witness*, p 416.
12. Hennessy, *The Prime Minister*, p 437.
13. Hennessy, *The Prime Minister*, p 438.

CHRONOLOGY

Year	Premiership
1990	28 November: John Major becomes Prime Minister, aged 47.
1991	January: Major agrees immediate attacks on Iraqi forces in Kuwait after expiry of UN deadline with President Bush. February: Operation Desert Storm defeats Iraqi army and liberates Kuwait in six days. British establish safe havens for Kurds in northern Iraq. Major meets Ian McKellen of Stonewall to discuss gay rights. VAT increased to 17.5%. Unpopular 'Poll Tax' replaced by Council Tax. December: Maastricht Treaty negotiations begin.
1992	February: Maastricht Treaty signed. 9 April: Conservatives win general election with majority of 21 seats. 16 September: 'Black Wednesday': sterling forced out of the European ERM. Conservative Party's economic reputation ruined. Prince Charles and Princess Diana legally separate. Lloyd's insurance market reveal losses of £2 billion. November: First British troops deployed to Bosnia.

History	Culture
East and West Germany sign reunification treaty. GDR ceases to exist.	Patricia Cornwell, *Post Mortem*. Ian McEwan, *The Innocent*. Films: *Goodfellas*. TV: *Have I Got News For You*.
Military structure of Warsaw Pact is dissolved. Parliament of Georgia votes to assert independence from USSR. Boris Yeltsin becomes first ever directly-elected president of Russian Federation. Bush and Gorbachev sign Strategic Arms Reduction Treaty. Peace accord ends 11-year civil war in El Salvador. Gorbachev resigns as President of USSR; the USSR officially ceases to exist. Legal framework for Apartheid in South Africa is destroyed.	Dummett, *The Logical Basis for Metaphysics*. Angela Carter, *Wise Children*. Brett Easton Ellis, *American Psycho*. John Grisham, *The Firm*. Madonna, *Sex*. John Updike, *Rabbit at Rest*. Dorfman, *Death and the Maiden*. Birtwistle, *Sir Gawain and the Green Knight* (opera). Nirvana, *Nevermind*. Films: *JFK. Silence of the Lambs. Thelma and Louise*.
Boutros Boutros Ghali becomes Secretary General of the UN. EC recognises Croatia and Slovenia as independent republics. Serb and federal army forces begin bombardment of Sarajevo after fighting escalates. Riots break out in LA after policemen are acquitted of beating a black motorist despite video evidence. UN condemns Serbs' 'ethnic cleansing' as war crime. Bill Clinton wins US presidential election.	J K Galbraith, *The Culture of Contentment*. Jung Chang, *Wild Swans*. Ian McEwan, *Black Dogs*. Michael Ondaatje, *The English Patient*. Damien Hirst, *The Physical Impossibility of Death in the Mind of Someone Living*. Whitney Houston, *I will always love you*. Kushner, *Angels in America*. Films: *Howard's End. Orlando. Strictly Ballroom*. TV: *Absolutely Fabulous*.

1993	February: Major's first meeting with US President Clinton.
	Chancellor Norman Lamont announces imposition of VAT on domestic fuel.
	March: Lamont removed as Chancellor.
	Government loses vote on Maastricht Treaty.
	December: Joint UK/Irish declaration to encourage talks in Northern Ireland.
1994	February: Homosexual age of consent reduced from 21 to 18.
	May: Sudden death of John Smith, leader of the Labour Party. July: Tony Blair succeeds him.
	August: IRA announces complete cessation of violence.
	November: National Lottery starts.

History	Culture
European Community's single market comes into force.	Margaret Thatcher, *The Downing Street Years*.
Terrorist bombing of World Trade Center in New York.	Andrew Motion, *Philip Larkin, A Writer's Life*.
UN security council declares 'safe areas' in Sarajevo, Tuzla, Zepa, Goradze, Bihac and Srebrenica in Bosnia-Herzigovina. Serbs later attack Srebrenica and Goradze.	Isabel Allende, *The Infinite Plain*. Roddy Doyle, *Paddy Clarke Ha Ha Ha*. Harold Pinter, *Moonlight*.
In Washington DC peace agreement is signed between Israel and the PLO.	Take That, *Take That and Party. Everything Changes*.
Maastricht treaty comes into force. European Community becomes European Union.	U2, *Zooropa*. Rachel Whiteread, *House*. Films: *Schindler's List. In the Name of the Father. Shadowlands*.
Silvio Berlusconi wins presidential election in Italy.	Hobsbawm, *Age of Extremes, The Short Twentieth Century*.
Nelson Mandela is sworn in as president of South Africa.	Joseph Heller, *Closing Time*. V S Naipaul, *A Way in the World*.
Israel withdraws military forces from the Jericho area of West Bank.	Arthur Miller, *Broken Glass*. Kurt Cobain of *Nirvana* commits suicide.
Israel and Jordan formally end their conflict.	Sistine Chapel's cleaning completed.
Russian forces invade Chechnya.	Films: *Forrest Gump. The Madness of King George. Pulp Fiction*.

1995 British and Irish governments present a framework document for Northern Ireland peace negotiations.

Tony Blair gets Labour Party to modify iconic Clause IV, the commitment to nationalisation, as move to 'New Labour'.

John Major stands for re-election as Conservative Party leader: John Redwood challenges him, and Major wins by only a slim majority.

December: first meetings between UK officials and the IRA.

1996 IRA breaks its cease-fire (in force since August 1994).

March: Dunblane massacre of schoolchildren leads to ban on private ownership of handguns.

EU bans export of British beef due to fears of transmitting BSE to humans as CJD.

1997 General election: New Labour wins landslide victory.

2 May: John Major leaves office after seven years and 155 days.

History	Culture
Austria, Finland and Sweden join the European Union.	Will Hutton, *The State We're In.*
UN troops withdraw from Somalia, unable to end civil war.	Martin Amis, *The Information.*
Cease-fire in Bosnia-Herzegovina (since Dec.1994) is broken. NATO launches air strikes against Serbs. Situation continues to escalate. New cease-fire agreement is announced. Peace talks are held near Dayton, USA.	Kate Atkinson, *Behind the Scenes at the Museum.*
	Timberlake Wertenbaker, *Break of Day.*
	Phillip Pullman, *Northern Lights.*
	The Beatles, *Anthology 1.*
	Britpop becomes popular (Blur, Oasis, etc)
Oklahoma City bombing in USA kills 166.	Moshe Safdie designs Library Square, Vancouver.
Israeli prime minister Yitzhak Rabin is assassinated in Tel Aviv.	Delmas Howe, *Liberty, Equality and Fraternity.*
Peace plan for Bosnia-Herzegovina signed in Paris.	Films: *Braveheart. Nixon. Sense and Sensibility.*

History	Culture
In first Palestinian general elections, Yassir Arafat is elected president.	Daniel Goldhagen, *Hitler's Willing Executioners.*
Boris Yeltsin inaugurated as Russian president after re-election.	T S Eliot, *Inventions of the March Hare, Poems.*
In Afghanistan, Taliban take over Kabul and impose Islamic law.	Luciano Berio, *Outis.*
Bill Clinton is re-elected as US president.	Jonathan Larson, *Rent.*
	Films: *William Shakespeare's Romeo and Juliet.. Trainspotting.*
	TV: *Changing Rooms. This Life.*

History	Culture
Kofi Annan replaces Butros Butros Ghali as UN Secretary General.	J K Rowling, *Harry Potter and the Philosopher's Stone.*
Israel withdraws troops from Hebron.	Films: *The Full Monty. Men in Black.*
	TV: *Teletubbies.*

FURTHER READING

John Major's own *Memoirs*, published in 1999 by Harper-Collins, London, are massive and revealing. The volume is one of the best written by any British 20th-century Prime Minister. Anthony Seldon's *Major: A Political Life*, published in 1997, was authorised and it is useful complement to Major's own memoirs. Three other more instant biographies are also evocative, highly readable and well researched: Bruce Anderson, *John Major: The Making of The Prime Minister* (Fourth Estate, London: 1991); Edward Pearce, *The Quiet Rise of John Major* (Weidenfeld & Nicolson, London: 1991), and Penny Junor *John Major; From Brixton to Downing Street* (Penguin, London: 1993 and 1996). Major's brother Terry Major-Ball wrote a delightful and affectionate volume about the family, *Major Major; Memories of An Older Brother* (Duckworth, London: 1994).

A number of his close Cabinet colleagues provide us with some insightful assessments of Major as Prime Minister. Chris Patten, *Not Quite The Diplomat* (Penguin, Allen Lane, London: 2005) and Douglas Hurd, *Memoirs* (Little, Brown, London: 2003) are by far the best. Another sympathetic portraits can be found in Ian Lang, *Blue Remembered Years* (Politico's, London: 2002). There is less insight in Michael Heseltine, *Life In The Jungle* (Coronet, London: 2000) Predictably there is more criticism to be found of Major in Norman Lamont, *In Office* (Warner Books, London: 1999) but he provides a well argued account of his life at the Treasury under Major. The views of one of Major's 'bastards' are also worth reading – John Redwood, *Singing The Blues* (Politico's, London: 2004).

Nigel Lawson in his massive *The View From Number Eleven* (Bantam Press, London: 1992) provides a useful assessment of Major as he rose from obscurity through the ranks of government. In *The Downing Street Years* (HarperCollins, London: 1993), Margaret Thatcher offers a more edgy and circumspect view of her former protégé. There are also a few sightings of Major in Nicholas Ridley's *Memoirs* (Fontana, London: 1998). Edwina Currie's *Diaries 1987–1992* (Time Warner, London: 2002) reveal another, unexpected side of Major's character.

Sarah Hogg and Jonathan Hill, *Too Close To Call; Power and Politics – John Major in No 10* (Warner Books, London: 1995) provides a vivid picture of life in his Policy Unit mostly during his first term as Prime Minister, the 1992 general election and his leadership contest in 1995. Matthew Parris, *Chance Witness; An Outsider's Life in Politics* (Penguin, London: 2003) offers some perceptive comments on Major. The most interesting diary of the Major years is by Gyles Brandreth, *Breaking The Code* (Weidenfeld & Nicolson, London: 1999). The best academic compilation of policy making in the Major government can be found in *The Major Effect*, edited by Dennis Kavanagh and Anthony Seldon (Macmillan, London: 1994).

There are sections on Major in some general histories of the Conservatives. The best are Robert Blake, *The Conservative Party from Peel to Major* (Heinemann, London: 1997), Ian Gilmour and Mark Ganett, *Whatever Happened to the Tories* (Fourth Estate, London: 1997) and John Ramsden, *An Appetite for Power* (HarperCollins, London: 1998). There are two insightful essays on Major in Peter Hennessy's *The Prime Minister: the Office and its Holders since 1945* (Penguin, London: 2000) and in Dick Leonard's, *A Century of Premiers: Salisbury to Blair* (Palgrave, London: 2005).

Two books on Northern Ireland are worth consulting for Major's role in the peace process. They are Eamonn Mallie and David McIntrick, *End Game in Ireland* (Hodder and Stoughton, London: 2002) and Dean Godson, *David Trimble and the Ordeal of Ulster Unionism* (HarperCollins, London: 2005).

PICTURE SOURCES

Page ix
John and Norma Major on a walkabout in Bath, 15 March 1997. (Courtesy Topham Picturepoint)

Pages 60–1
The US President Bill Clinton and John Major pictured at a press conference at Chequers, 4 June 1994. (Courtesy Topham Picturepoint)

Page 127
John Major photographed at The Oval Cricket Ground the day of his election defeat, 2 May 1997. (Courtesy Topham Picturepoint)

INDEX

A

Adams, Gerry 93, 95, 97
Aitken, Jonathan 105
Al Fayed, Mohammed
    105
Anderson, Bruce 1
Archer, Jeffrey 52
Ashcroft, Lord 120

B

Baldwin, Stanley 29
Balfour, Arthur 3, 74
Barber, Tony 9
Bell, Steve 2
Blair, Tony viii, 1, 2,
    38, 76, 109, 116–17,
    126
Blunkett, David 116
Bonar Law, Andrew 3
Brandreth, Gyles 118, 121,
    124
Brooke, Peter 10, 93
Brown, Gordon 86, 117
Bruce-Gardyne, Jock 10
Bush, George (Senior)
    40–2, 91, 92
Butler, David 113
Butler, R A 74

C

Callaghan, James 121
Cameron, David 63, 126
Campbell, Alistair 106,
    109
Chamberlain, Neville 3
Churchill, Sir Winston S 86
Clarke, Kenneth 65, 66, 68,
    70, 80, 83, 112
Clinton, Bill 89, 90–2, 97,
    100
Cranborne, Robert 125
Currie, Edwina 25–6, 29,
    20, 34, 104

D

Disraeli, Benjamin 74
Douglas-Home, Sir Alec 3
Douro, Lord 10
Duncan Smith, Iain 79, 120
Dykes, Hugh 112

E

Ecclestone, Bernie 116
Eden, Sir Anthony 83

F

Fowler, Norman 13

G

George, Eddie 67
Gilmour, Sir Ian 25
Goldsmith, Sir James 65
Gummer, John 66

H

Hague, William 120
Hamilton, Neil 105
Haselhurst, Alan 10
Heath, Edward 3, 9, 20, 112
Heseltine, Michael 16, 20–1, 24, 36–7, 38, 62, 68, 70, 82, 83, 106, 112, 121, 122
Hill, Jonathan 26, 45, 47, 58, 67, 110
Hogg, Sarah 26, 45
Horam, John 111
Howard, Michael 10, 66, 78, 79, 111, 115, 120
Howe, Sir Geoffrey 16, 18, 19
Hurd, Douglas 16, 21, 35, 36, 37, 48, 62, 68, 87, 89, 106, 108, 112, 121

I

Ingham, Bernard 108

J

Jopling, Michael 11

Jowell, Tessa 116

K

Kavanagh, Denis 113
Kinnock, Neil 57
Knight, Jill 9
Kohl, Helmut 45, 64, 68

L

Lamont, Norman 37, 66, 68, 80, 117, 120
Lang, Ian 37, 62, 116
Lawson, Nigel 11, 13–15, 17, 18, 19, 66, 70
Leigh-Pemberton, Robin 67
Lilley, Peter 10, 72, 111
Lipton, Colonel Marcus 7
Liverpool, Lord 3
Livingstone, Ken 9

M

MacDonald, J Ramsay 5
Macleod, Ian 24
Macmillan, Harold 85
Major, Norma (wife) 9, 24
Major, Pat (sister) 69
Major, Terry (brother) 6
Major, Tom (father) 5
Mandelson, Peter 106, 116
Mates, Michael 105
Mayhew, Patrick 11
McGuinness, Martin 93, 95, 96

McKellen, Ian 34
Mellor, David 37, 105
Merchant, Piers 105
Meyer, Chris 108
Middleton, Sir Peter 18
Milligan, Stephen 105
Mills, David 116
Milosevic, Slobodan 88, 89
Mitchell, George 100
Molyneaux, Jim 96, 99
Murdoch, Rupert 106

N
Nadir, Asil 105
Newton, Tony 13
Nolan, Lord 106

O
Oborne, Peter 109
O'Donnell, Gus 48, 108
Orwell, George 29
Owen, David 88

P
Paice, James 111
Parris, Matthew 1, 31, 37, 122
Patten, Chris 10, 25, 34, 48, 62, 107–8
Portillo, Michael 72
Powell, Charles 16, 35
Powell, J Enoch 1
Prescott, John 116

R
Raison, Timothy 11
Redwood, John 65, 72, 107, 110
Renton, Sir David 10
Reynolds, Albert 95
Ridley, Nicholas 23
Rifkind, Michael 37, 87
Rosebery, Lord 3
Ryder, Sir Richard 37

S
Saddam Hussein 17, 40–2
Salisbury, Lord vii
Scargill, Arthur 83
Schlesinger, Helmut 67
Scott, Sir Richard 105
Seldon, Anthony 69, 82, 91, 118
Smith, John 57
Smith, Tim 105

T
Tapsell, Peter 124
Taylor, Ian 112
Tebbit, Norman 53, 71
Thatcher, Denis 12
Thatcher, Margaret viii, 2, 3, 10, 12–13, 15, 16, 18, 19–21, 23, 24, 33–4, 38, 44, 52, 53, 58, 85, 116
Trimble, David 99

V
Vance, Cyrus 88

W
Wakeham, John 11
Walters, Sir Alan 17
Williams, Hywel 107

Y
Yeo, Tim 105
Young, Lord 84

THE 20 BRITISH PRIME MINISTERS
OF THE 20TH CENTURY

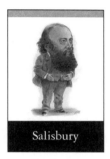

Salisbury

SALISBURY

Conservative politician, prime minister
1885–6, 1886–92 and 1895–1902, and
the last to hold that office in the House
of Lords.
by Eric Midwinter
Visiting Professor of Education at
Exeter University
ISBN 1-904950-54-X (pb)

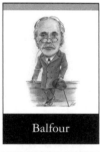

Balfour

BALFOUR

Balfour wrote that Britain favoured 'the
establishment in Palestine of a national
home for the Jewish people', the so-
called 'Balfour Declaration'.
by Ewen Green
of Magdalen College Oxford
ISBN 1-904950-55-8 (pb)

Campbell-
Bannerman

CAMPBELL-BANNERMAN

Liberal Prime Minister, who started the
battle with the Conservative-dominated
House of Lords.
by Lord Hattersley
former Deputy Leader of the Labour
Party and Cabinet member in Wilson
and Callaghan's governments.
ISBN 1-904950-56-6 (pb)

Asquith

ASQUITH

His administration laid the foundation of Britain's welfare state, but he was plunged into a major power struggle with the House of Lords.

by Stephen Bates

a senior correspondent for the *Guardian*.

ISBN 1-904950-57-4 (pb)

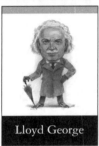

Lloyd George

LLOYD GEORGE

By the end of 1916 there was discontent with Asquith's management of the war, and Lloyd George schemed secretly with the Conservatives in the coalition government to take his place.

by Hugh Purcell

television documentary maker.

ISBN 1-904950-58-2 (pb)

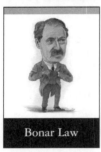

Bonar Law

BONAR LAW

In 1922 he was the moving spirit in the stormy meeting of Conservative MPs which ended the coalition, created the 1922 Committee and reinstated him as leader.

by Andrew Taylor

Professor of Politics at the University of Sheffield.

ISBN 1-904950-59-0 (pb)

Baldwin

BALDWIN

Baldwin's terms of office included two major political crises, the General Strike and the Abdication.

by Anne Perkins

a journalist, working mostly for the *Guardian*, as well as a historian of the British labour movement.

ISBN 1-904950-60-4 (pb)

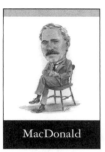

MacDonald

MACDONALD

In 1900 he was the first secretary of the newly formed Labour Representation Committee (the original name for the Labour party). Four years later he became the first Labour prime minister.

by Kevin Morgan

who teaches government and politics at Manchester University.
ISBN 1-904950-61-2 (pb)

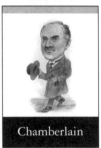

Chamberlain

CHAMBERLAIN

His name will forever be linked to the policy of appeasement and the Munich agreement he reached with Hitler.

by Graham Macklin

manager of the research service at the National Archives.
ISBN 1-904950-62-0 (pb)

Churchill

CHURCHILL

Perhaps the most determined and inspirational war leader in Britain's history.

by Chris Wrigley

who has written about David Lloyd George, Arthur Henderson and W E Gladstone.
ISBN 1-904950-63-9 (pb)

Attlee

ATTLEE

His post-war government enacted a broad programme of socialist legislation in spite of conditions of austerity. His legacy: the National Health Service.

by David Howell

Professor of Politics at the University of York and an expert in Labour's history.
ISBN 1-904950-64-7 (pb)

Eden

EDEN

His premiership will forever be linked to the fateful Suez Crisis.

by Peter Wilby

former editor of the *New Statesman*.
ISBN 1-904950-65-5 (pb)

Macmillan

MACMILLAN

He repaired the rift between the USA and Britain created by Suez and secured for Britain co-operation on issues of nuclear defence, but entry into the EEC was vetoed by de Gaulle in 1963.

by Francis Beckett

author of BEVAN, published by Haus in 2004.
ISBN 1-904950-66-3 (pb)

Douglas-Home

DOUGLAS-HOME

Conservative politician and prime minister 1963-4, with a complex career between the two Houses of Parliament.

by David Dutton

who teaches History at Liverpool University.
ISBN 1-904950-67-1 (pb)

Wilson

WILSON

He held out the promise progress, of 'the Britain that is going to be forged in the white heat of this revolution'. The forced devaluation of the pound in 1967 frustrated the fulfilment of his promises.

by Paul Routledge

The *Daily Mirror's* chief political commentator.
ISBN 1-904950-68-X (pb)

Heath

HEATH

A passionate European, he succeeded during his premiership in effecting Britain's entry to the EC.

by Denis MacShane

Minister for Europe in Tony Blair's first government.

ISBN 1-904950-69-8 (pb)

Callaghan

CALLAGHAN

His term in office was dominated by industrial unrest, culminating in the 'Winter of Discontent'.

by Harry Conroy

When James Callaghan was Prime Minister, Conroy was the Labour Party's press officer in Scotland, and he is now editor of the Scottish *Catholic Observer*.

ISBN 1-904950-70-1 (pb)

Thatcher

THATCHER

Britain's first woman prime minister and the longest serving head of government in the 20th century (1979–90), but also the only one to be removed from office in peacetime by pressure from within her own party.

by Clare Beckett

teaches social policy at Bradford University.

ISBN 1-904950-71-X (pb)

Major

MAJOR

He enjoyed great popularity in his early months as prime minister, as he seemed more caring than his iron predecessor, but by the end of 1992 nothing seemed to go right.

by Robert Taylor

is Research Associate at the LSE's Centre for Economic Performance.

ISBN 1-904950-72-8 (pb)

Blair

BLAIR

He is therefore the last prime minister of the 20th century and one of the most controversial ones, being frequently accused of abandoning cabinet government and introducing a presidential style of leadership.

by Mick Temple

is a senior lecturer in Politics and Journalism at Staffordshire University.

ISBN 1-904950-73-6 (pb)

THE 20 BRITISH PRIME MINISTERS OF THE 20TH CENTURY

www.hauspublishing.co.uk

TITO
by Neil Barnett
ISBN 1-904950-31-0 (pb)

Tall, strikingly handsome, powerfully charismatic, the young Croatian motor engineer called Josip Broz was the kind of man you noticed – but only when he wanted you to notice him.

'He had the knack', writes Neil Barnett, biographer of the man who would become Tito, 'of fading into the background to avoid trouble, yet at the same time coming to the fore to demonstrate his abilities.'

These were qualities that served him well as a secret revolutionary Communist, underground and on the run for much of the 1930s, and served him again when outnumbered and outgunned, his Partisans fought the Germans and their Balkan allies through the Second World War.

Barnett traces Tito's long personal road from Moscow Communist to patriotic revolutionary. It was an identity shift that many others would have liked to achieve: that Tito alone defied Stalin to his face and survived built a unique mystique. It was a mystique that was powerful enough to invent the country called Yugoslavia.

Tito used that authority to build the unitary Yugoslavia out of disparate and competing territories and ethnic groups, employing a mixture of persuasion and vicious repression. His achievement was that his Yugoslavia remained stable for so long. The tragedy was that when Tito ended – overweight, and grotesquely festooned with medals and distinctions he had awarded himself – Yugoslavia ended too. It was a country that could only be contained by his personal prestige, writes Barnett: perhaps uniquely in 20th century Europe, Tito's personality is the most important clue to his country's history.

RABIN
by Linda Benedikt
ISBN 1-904950-06-X (pb)

He was dubbed 'Mr Security' by his countrymen, yet Yitzhak Rabin (1922–1995) was murdered for what he ultimately failed to deliver: security. It seems that only in death did he become the symbol of what could have been possible: a just peace between Israel and the Palestinians.

Rabin became a soldier by chance and necessity rather than by choice. He spent nearly his entire life fighting Israel's wars against Arabs and Palestinians. His natural talent for strategic thinking, deep analysis and detachment from the political game, placed him first at the top of the Israeli military and later political echelons. He was an admired Chief of Staff, an unorthodox ambassador, a dedicated Defence Minister and twice led his country as Prime Minister.

After the first Palestinian uprising in the late 1980s sent shockwaves through the country, he started to realise that Israel could not win this war by force. Upon his re-election as Prime Minister in 1992 he instigated a diplomatic process to end the conflict. Tragically his lack of political vision, his deep-rooted ambivalence towards the Palestinians, together with his cautious instinct prevented him from fully implementing the peace process for which he was ultimately murdered in 1995 and for which he is still remembered today.